TRANSFORMING
INDIAN
MANAGERS

THROUGH **PROJECTIVE METHODOLOGY**

I0490459

Prof. Indira J Parikh
Dr. Bharti Venkatesh

INDIA · SINGAPORE · MALAYSIA

Notion Press

No.8, 3rd Cross Street,
CIT Colony, Mylapore,
Chennai, Tamil Nadu – 600004

First Published by Notion Press 2020
Copyright © Prof. Indira J Parikh & Dr. Bharti Venkatesh 2020
All Rights Reserved.

ISBN 978-1-64899-693-1

CONTENTS

Acknowledgments.. 5

Testimonials.. 11

Synopsis of the Book... 13

Synopsis of Chapter 1 - History of the Growth of Indian
Organizations 17

Chapter 1: History of Growth of Indian Organizations 19

Synopsis of Chapter 2 - Storytelling as a Methodology of
Learning and Development 45

Chapter 2: Storytelling as a Methodology of Learning and
Development 47

Synopsis of Chapter 3 - Stories by Managers 71

Chapter 3: Stories by Managers 73

Synopsis of Chapter 4 - Findings And Conclusions from
The Stories: What do the Stories Tell?..............................123

Chapter 4: Profile of Senior Managers.................................125

Synopsis of Chapter 5 - Organizational Maturity Perspective
for Tomorrow...163

Chapter 5: Organizational Maturity Perspective for
Tomorrow..165

Summary of the Book..173

References 179

Figures Adapted From..183

Tables Adapted From 185

ACKNOWLEDGMENTS

This book has had many breaks and interruptions. It has taken six years to complete from the time it was visualized as a possibility of an idea. It started out as an effort to put together all the concepts and frameworks which had evolved during the assignments with organizations which were then called the training programs and or management development programs. These were later started to be called as Learning and Development programs for managers across levels of the organization. Many new names were also given by different organizations. These programs provided insights into the changing scenarios in the economic environment of the country and the transformations occurring in the Indian organizations. It provided the transforming profiles of Indian managers across sectors as the managers and organizations grappled with new challenges and constantly respond to the new demands from the organization and environment.

The role of leadership was also transforming at a pace unparalleled before. It was the leadership's search for preparing employees to the new challenges of growth through new models of learning and working with perspectives that I was invited to initiate Organization Design and Development work with organizations. It was also to prepare the employees to visualize the new scenario of global economy. The opportunity to work with the totality of the organizations and the senior HR managers as well as top management contributed immensely and provided us clarity and understanding of the organizational and employee issues encountered by the organizations.

The concepts which have been developed while working with organizations is also the contribution of the CEOs, MDs and other HR professionals with whom discussions took place and search for models of learning which would be meaningful and relevant to the emerging scenarios. These frameworks not only had to be relevant to the people of the organization, but they also had to show results in the balance sheet of the organization. With many of the organization it turned out to be an enduring association of three to nine years evolving relevant concepts and frameworks. Over time these became the guiding force in deciding new models of learning and developmental inputs.

I take this opportunity to thank first three organizations which invited me and contributed to my evolving as an OD consultant. The first major breakthrough came from Indian Oil Corporation and then State Bank of India subsequently. Mahindra and Mahindra Tractor Division, Onida, Zydus Cadilla. Anil Products Ltd. Force Motors, Monopol Intech and several other organizations. The ones listed here are the organizations from which I have used extensive data and conceptual frameworks. The CEOs who trusted me with the use of the new models and conceptual frameworks were of immense support and spent time to discuss and share their perspectives. To name a few, Mr. K.J. Davasia of MTD now known as Farm Equipment Sector, Mr. Pankaj Patel of Zydus Cadila. Mr. Gulu Mirchandani, Mr. Sonu Mirchandani and Mr. Vijay Mansukhani of Onida. Mr. Parmanand Parekh, Mrs. Sarlaben Parekh and Mr. Nayan Parekh of Monopol Intech and Mr. Abhay Firodia of Force Motors. Two other names were significant Mr. Krishnamurthy of Mudra Communications. I have benefited immensely from their reflections and responses to the efforts as a consultant to facilitate in transforming their organizations. These were some of the giants of the industries riding the waves of growth and on their own creating some big waves of growth.

As the book has taken such a long time I take this opportunity to convey and acknowledge my appreciation to Bharati Venkatesh who was then Bharati Kollan who started to put the consultancy reports together. She displayed immense patience and persistence in holding on to the manuscript and kept pursuing the discussions to put it together.

The book also got delayed with simultaneous family issues of my husband's health, the setting up of FLAME and passing away of my husband. All these and many other emerging realities of life space and multiple roles continued to contribute to delays.

But one fine morning that moment of decision had arrived which made it possible to pick up the manuscript and said now or it will never happen. By this time as I read the manuscript, I realized that though the data of the times was correct and that was the reality then, the times had taken a quantum leap and hop scotched into a different decade zone and the reference point was a new century. Keeping that in mind, the manuscript had to be re looked and understood in the continuity of the past and the present. From the time it began to be documented, to the time it is finally written the manuscript has undergone significant changes to finally be considered a book.

The book is for managers, this book is for organizations, this book is for management students and the OD facilitators and the practitioners. The understanding transition provides insights into the transforming work cultures, the transforming organizations, and the world of employees as they grapple with the new realities of their lives, the organizations and the society. The intertwining of the two realities on multiple axes of the social system, the social roles and relationships, the work organizations and the work roles and relationships puts all employees on a crucible of delivery and performance and enhancing their quality of life. In this context the development of perspective and the broader experience and exposure to present realities of global environment becomes very important. Sometimes a simple statement of a broader perspective provides a whole new direction for life and approach to work life. If this book provides insights even to a few employees and few organizations, which would make their life and organization space a more dynamic space it would give us the satisfaction of meaningful effort.

Many have contributed to writing of this book. I take this moment to thank IIMA for providing an environment to engage with organizations fully believing in the philosophy that the experience of working with industry creates better teachers and faculty. Ms. J.S. VijayaPiriya who worked with me for fifteen years was familiar with my writing and ways of working to keep rewriting many times over. Her patience and smiling face never complained, but appreciated that the writing of course conveyed more each time.

Joining FLAME in 2005, the book was on hold for some time with starting of FLAME with its new concept of Liberal Education. All pangs of creation of an institution took its own time and again put the book on hold. As life settled down, Bharti kept pursuing that we should complete the almost completed book and so the manuscript was once again restarted to finally put it all together. Here Pragati Chopra and now Pragati Shah and Sahana Mukherjee contributed immensely to type the manuscript several times. Kamya Pahwa joined as research assistant specially to help convert manuscript into a book. With her patience and soft speaking style continued the pressure, to complete the book. These are young women dedicated to their growth who believed that the book should be completed. Sudheer Chhotalal from FLAME library provided support in help identify recent trends in research on this theme and found some excellent references to make the book more relevant to the scholars as well as students of present times.

In all of this I share my appreciation of FLAME which is a place and a space of the campus which evokes an experience and a language of writing. FLAME is a space where in the midst of the hustle and bustle of young students one can withdraw into oneself to pursue the writing.

One of the basic philosophy and value of FLAME is to encourage research and promote publications. This approach has also supported me in the working on this book. Despite many demands of running and managing campus, the journey of completing this book has not been easy. Many institutions and memories are tied to this book.

The book has been lingering for the last five years after I left FLAME. In the mean time we always felt that the book was become obsolete.

But as the book is based on Projective Technique, in any given point of time, individual and organization keep consisting dilemma of membership in organization, definition and meaning of task, job and role, relationship and interface across the hierarchy and working in groups. These some core issues are faced by managers and organization. There will be some people who still be grappling the issues of yesterday and today. They would need some clarity to move forward. This book provides insight into this group of people who can be mobilized to understand themselves and move from their managerial location to take leadership role.

We would like to express our sense of appreciation to Notion Press for accepting our book. We would also like to thank Notion Press team especially Vignesh and Sherine for helping and guiding us with the new technology.

Prof. Indira J. Parikh
Dr. Bharti Venkatesh

TESTIMONIALS

Arun Nabar - Founder at Spectra Interventions

Prof. Indira Parikh was engaged as a consultat for "Organizational Culture Change" program at Mahindra Tractors, mid 1996 onwards. She used multiple interventions in various workshops deisgned for senior and middle level managers. TAT as in instrument helped me realise my potential, pulls and pushes of goal settings, drive towards achievement of the goal set, my patterns of relatedness with authority figures, my willingness to seek help from various stakeholders, withholding of myself when in group settings and inner dynamic of feelings and thoughts that impact action choices. I believe TAT was on intervention that made me make a choice and enabled to start and run successfully a management consulting firm (Spectra Interventions) after 3 years.

Dr. Rajesh Save – (Ex Global HR Head Syntel)

Though I had studied TAT (Thematic Apperception Test) as a part of my syllabus, it was a fresh experience when I took it again after a decade during my M and M tendure. More thatn "What" it was "How" and "Why" of personality that gave me penetrating insight into my "unexplained behavior" that was hidden in blind self. The interpretation was so powerful that even after over 20 years, I still remember as if it happened yesterday. More than the tool what mattered was the succinct processing of information which was adroitly done. Thanks to Indira Ma'am and Raghu, we all found the entire intervention unique and discerning and therefore effective and created far-reaching imprint on our minds.

SYNOPSIS OF THE BOOK

This book is all about transformations. The story began when the country was in the upheaval of change. 'Change' was all about organizations craving for opportunities to grow, challenges to cope with the opening up of the economy, trying to run the race when they have felt tied down, entering an environment wished for but unable to enter and trying to swim against the flow. 'Change' was the buzz word, changing economies both national and global were an experienced reality and all that was known and familiar seemed to be outdated and obsolete. Organizations and managers grappled with the transformations required in the employees across levels to respond to the changing business landscape of the organizations and to help them acquire skills and role orientations that would strengthen the organizations to run the race.

It is in this context and backdrop of changing national scenarios that organizations initiated and attempted Organization Development and Design Developmental inputs to facilitate managerial responses to the changing business scenario. Generally, organizations have developmental or training inputs for some of the managers who are sent to training programs that are perceived and experienced either as a punishment to leave their jobs to go and travel for such programs or a reward to go to a good institution or hotel to learn and enjoy. Some, of course, experienced the training programs as a time to invest in themselves for growth and prepare themselves with knowledge, attitudes and skills for future positions and/or change of designation or positional responsibilities.

This was also a time when the focus of training and development was shifting to learning and development. New frameworks of learning were emerging to respond to the requirements of the organizations as well as managers to take newer and larger roles as the process of expansion and growth were accelerating at a pace not known before. The learning and development focus also brought out a more holistic emphasis on preparing employees across levels of the organizations. It was no more the top and senior people who were being prepared but employees across the organization were required to prepare themselves for the dramatic technological innovations which were beginning to make their appearance. These innovations would change lifestyles and ways of working, the glimpses of which were beginning to be felt across the country and globally.

Organizations were moving from small scale and medium enterprises to large, mammoth and global organizations. Indian organizations were entering partnerships, alliances, strategic alliances, mergers and acquisitions and public-private partnerships. The mobility of employees was happening at a dizzying pace. New industries were beginning to appear on the business landscape of the country. New names in leadership roles were beginning to reverberate on the Indian organizational scenario. And a whole new concept of managers and managerial roles were beginning to be sought after in the world of organizations.

It is at a configuration of the evolution of the Indian business environment, Indian industry, Indian organizations, employees of Indian organizations, the introduction of newer technologies, IT revolution and the whole of mobile, laptops, Facebook, twitter, I-pods, I-pads and similar other inventions. The other dimensions of the configuration are the malls, retail environment of branded and other goods and the multicultural cuisine available both in rural and urban India. All these create a unique juxtaposition where people in general and employees of work organizations need to transform themselves to respond and integrate with the emerging reality of India.

It is in this kaleidoscope of Indian landscape that many organizations in the late eighties and nineties realized the need for a holistic approach to investing in their managers. Parikh's work with Indian organizations and Indian managers and the transformations occurring in Indian organizations became a starting point to study the whole organization and to explore the possibilities of what were the hurting spots in the organization and why. The people in the organizations had brought the organizations this far and most had done well given the context in which they were operating. Now was the time for propelling the organization to a different level of growth and with the people they had or bring in additional people through recruitment and slowly but certainly start transforming the existing organization work culture. It was time to move forward, it was time for transforming employees to help them discover their potential and to translate organizational potential to a growth path and to success and excellence. The time for Indian organizations had come to crystallize their work identity and to emerge as contributing to the growth of the economy.

The book explores through a storytelling methodology the process of transformation initiated by organizations through a holistic approach of learning and development of their employees across three levels of management—junior, middle and senior. The organizations were all concerned with growth, expansion, the introduction of new technology and people who were in the organization for decades. Most of the employees did not have the experience of other organizations, nor had they the exposure required to perceive the kind of transformations required. They were men devoted to their jobs, they knew the job they had done for long and were confused and perplexed at the changes occurring in the external environment. Their aspirations were rising, their need to move forward was increasing, their willingness to propel the organization forward was high and their participation to be part of the new environment was immense.

SYNOPSIS OF CHAPTER 1 - HISTORY OF THE GROWTH OF INDIAN ORGANIZATIONS

With the opening up of the economy from the seventies to the nineties, Indian organizations experienced pulls and pushes from a different kind of economic governance. As new competitors were entering into the country, the Indian industry went in for collaborations and joint ventures, partnerships, alliances and mergers. The Indian organizations imported technology from many countries. With this came their personnel, work culture, work ethics and their ways of running an industry. Indian organizations also borrowed structures, management practices and systems from the west and superimposed them on the existing structures. However, the ground for this was not prepared and Indian organizations began to experience and encounter flux and transition. The business environment of all Indian organizations changed significantly and this impacted the working within the organization. Moreover, people were not prepared for these new initiatives to move from a traditional, familial, personalized affiliation-related work culture to a more task and function-oriented formalized work culture of a higher competitive and complex environment.

In this flux and transition, there was an overall awareness of loss, a restlessness within the organization and senior management leadership, which generated anxiety, apprehension and a need for action. It was in such times that an OD (organization development) intervention was needed to facilitate the renewal of both the employees and the organizations. This chapter takes account of the OD interventions which contributed to evolving an alignment of and a shared understanding of action choices to facilitate the organization to become vibrant and dynamic as well as to respond to the emerging opportunities and challenges.

CHAPTER I

HISTORY OF GROWTH OF INDIAN ORGANIZATIONS

Introduction

Indian society for the last 2500 years has been dominantly an agrarian society. The path of industrialization worldwide goes back to more than 200 years and in India, it can be stretched back to more than 100 years. For the first 70 of those 100 years, the country was intensely occupied in struggling for independence. In the first 30 years of the next 50 years (from the fifties to the seventies) of independence, the country opted for a form of economic governance that would make the country self-reliant and an industrially viable nation. In the next 20 years (from the seventies to the nineties) there was a push for a different form of economic governance.

With the opening up of the economy and the new competitors coming into the country, the Indian industries and organizations went in for enthusiastic collaborations and joint ventures, partnerships, strategic alliances and mergers. The Indian organizations borrowed technology from Japan, the US, UK, Europe and Korea and as well as many other countries. With the technology from other countries came their personnel, work culture, work ethics, organization structures and their ways of operating industry and modes of interfacing with the environment and work relationships. The impact of the transfer of technology has been the study of many researchers. {Baumgartel, H. (1983); Small, B.W. (1977); Pearson, C.A.L/Chatterjee S.R. (1999), James, P.N/ Mathur.

A/ Zhang Yong (2000)}. The Indian organizations also borrowed structures, management practices and systems from the multinational organizations and their parent countries and superimposed them on the existing structures of Indian organizations. The Indian organizations invited multinational consultants from many western countries to redesign the Indian organization structures, management practices, management systems and national, international and global business strategies. Both the borrowing of technology and governance as well as the new organization vision provided the Indian CEOs and the organizations their dreams and new aspirations to chase.

The dreams and aspirations generated by the consultative processes mobilized the CEOs, the heads and senior managers to make their organizations grow and become highly successful organizations. They started to weave these dreams and aspirations into a personal vision, an organization mission, policies and strategies to be translated into results and targets dramatically different than the ones which had existed earlier. The HR and personnel function was mobilized to translate these into targets, KRAs for each of the employees and the senior management waited for the results to follow. However, the employees and the organization started to lag. The large number of employees and the rest of the organization could not follow, nor keep pace with the new vision, aspirations, expectations, and demands of the CEOs. Moreover, a very large number of employees overnight began to experience a fall in self-esteem, a lack of self-worth and a feeling of being devalued by the same entrepreneurs and leaders who valued them earlier for their contribution to the growth of the organization. Researchers on self-attitudes and esteem of employees have drawn much attention with specific reference to cross-cultural implications and the emerging consequences of fast-paced growth and transformations {Burger, P.C. and Doktor, B. 1976; Deva, S. 1979; Arbose. J. 1982, Falkenberg, A; Glamheden, H.; Agrawal, N.; Chong, L.-C. 2004}.

Growth of Indian Organizations

Indian organizations began to experience and encounter flux and transition more significantly in the last three decades, the 70s to 2000 and then from 2000 onwards (Boseman, F.G. 1975). In order to understand the nature of this transition, we must look at the country's social as well as organizational context.

1. India experienced and continues to experience growth and development simultaneously but at differential paces in industrial and social sectors. The industrial sector is growing at a much faster pace than the social sector. The social sector with its deeply embedded attitudes, beliefs and values anchored largely in the agrarian rural sector initially brought to the workplace by the people in the organization. This creates a process lag within the functioning of the organization. The society, as well as the industries, carry historical baggage of 2500 years of role-taking and interfaces deeply rooted in social structures and hierarchy, whereas the policies of industrial growth and development are designed and based on global and international considerations. These demand and necessitate a different way of working and relating in the work organization. The employees have to shift from a social mode of relating to a formal functional role-taking and interfacing around tasks, goals and objectives.

2. In India, there is a diversity of ownership of industry, size of organizations, complexity of technology and organizations reflecting different stages phases of growth.

3. There is an overwhelmingly powerful socio-cultural milieu that influences the family which, in turn, impacts the role-taking of the individuals in social settings as well as in organizations. The cultural and social structures are carried over to formal work organizations. Pulls and pushes of both the traditional relationships' patterns and the professional expectations of a task and work culture impact both social and formal roles of individuals (Garg. P.K. and Parikh, I.J. 1986)

21

4. The socialization process of the family fosters the emotive maps to be anchored in social structures whereas the socialization and induction processes of organizations foster cognitive and logical and rational maps anchored in formal task structures (Parikh, I.J. 1988).

5. Socialization from educational systems and work organizations gives rise to a new set of emotive and cognitive maps anchored in aspirations of occupations and professionalism. Both these systems then pull and push the individual in opposite directions for role performance. The emotive and cognitive maps of the primary system viz. the family, society and culture, however, have more enduring roots (Parikh, I.J. 1988; Pearson, Cecil A.L/ Chatterjee Samir R. 2000).

6. With the transformations occurring in life spaces of people there is a simultaneous shift in attitudes, values, beliefs and modes of meeting life situations both at home and work. This creates a unique juxtaposition of the old and the new and the modern and the traditional (Garg, Pulin K, and Parikh, I.J, 1986 Pearson, Cecil A.L/Chatterjee Samir R. 1999; Das T.K. 2001).

Internal and external environment of Indian organizations: Impact of new technology and management practices

The business environment of all Indian organizations has changed significantly. This has impacted the workings within the organizations. Similarly, the social environment of society and culture have also undergone and are undergoing changes. This accelerates the change within and outside.

Figure 1 presents the transformations in the business environment and its impact on both the external and the internal environments of organizations.

Figure 1: People-Environment of Organizations

i. Indian organizations have worked for a long time with family culture enclosed in social structures

ii. The organization culture is influenced by external environment through new and/or younger people who reflect the transformations occurring in the culture and society

iii. The internal environment is influenced by groups of people, management practices and task interfaces which have existed for a long time and the new processes resulting from growth

iv. The external environment continuously transforms itself through competitiveness in the market and impacts the internal environment of the organizations

{Parikh, Indira .J, Organization Cultural Transformation Process, A Study of Mahindra & Mahindra Tractor Division, Indian Institute of Management (Ahmedabad), (Jan – May 1997)}

Figure 1 suggests that both the internal and external environments of Indian organizations are simultaneously undergoing a transformation.

The pace of change has substantially accelerated in the last decades. This pulls and pushes the internal environment of the organization and the employees especially the younger generation in many directions (Bamel U.K, Rangnekar S. & Rastogi R. 2011). What was once considered the asset and strength of Indian family-owned organizations, viz. the family culture of a large joint family in an organization started to be considered a liability and a piece of baggage (Parikh, Indira.J, and Rath, Laura, 1998). This became more pronounced as competition increased and the results and performance contributed to the survival of the organization.

Organizations introduced new technology, new organization structures, and management practices. However, the ground for planting these new processes was not prepared. Moreover, nor were the people prepared for these new initiatives to move from one context of a traditional, familial, personalized affiliation-related work culture to a more task and function-oriented formalized work culture. Somehow, it was assumed that the borrowed culture was good for the organization and so people must follow and would follow. However, this did not happen. In fact, most employees in organizations nostalgically held on to the past and talked of the earlier work culture, the personalized relationships and accessibility of the owner-managers. They carried feelings of identification, belonging and ownership with the progenitor's owner-managers and the organization. This nostalgia, in fact, inhibited the shift of people to move to the more formal, functional role and task processes.

Figure 2 presents the past and the present environment of organizations.

As the opportunities emerged, the organizations began to make choices and strategic decisions for growth. Some opted for BPR— Business Process Reengineering, while some others opted for state-of-the-art technology and some opted for mergers and acquisitions. All this created and contributed to the new steps and phases of growth. This growth also created upheavals, turmoil and turbulence both within and outside the organizations.

Figure 2: Business Environment of Indian Organizations

i.   Internal organization consists of organization culture, history of growth, cumulative past and long standing relationships and association and traditional meaning of work as duty and karma

ii. The external environment of the past was of sellers' market and monopoly with the focus on self reliance as well as national priority of creating employment opportunities for large numbers of people

iii. Internal environment of the present meant growth new structures and as such new definition of managerial roles and changes in the mode of working

iv. In the present, change is inevitable both in the internal as well as external environment and the challenge is the survival of the fittest or biggest

{Parikh, Indira .J, Organization Cultural Transformation Process, A Study of Mahindra & Mahindra Tractor Division, Indian Institute of Management (Ahmedabad), (Jan – May 1997)}

The interplay of the internal and external environment confronts both people and organizations to move from the existing traditional and familial work culture to a newly emerging focus on professional work culture. The past provided stability whereas the present provides new challenges and opportunities (Parikh, Indira.J, 1998).

Figure 2 suggests that the flux in both the internal and external business environments makes it necessary for Indian organizations and their leadership to respond to the transformation with clarity and directionality. The owner-manager became the CEOs and the top management began to bring a new vision and design process is to foster a new work culture.

The Indian organizations do carry the baggage of historical past of the socio-cultural context of Indian joint families (Garg, Pulin.K, and Parikh, Indira.J, 1986). However, this baggage also had its strengths from which grew large and mammoth organizations, from one-man-entrepreneur and enterprise to industries and industrial empires which created self-reliance (on indigenous products). As such, the employees working in organizations with such entrepreneurs had role models and brought their sincerity, loyalty and dedication to their work.

The transformation of an individual, system, organization, industry, society, family and culture are inevitable processes of life and living. The only difference is that in the agrarian tradition of India the transformation was slow and steady providing stability and continuity to both the people and society. As such, the nature of work and social living were well-integrated, punctuated only by natural or man-made disasters arising out of caste, class and clan conflicts. Today, however, the pace of change is so fast that the obsoleteness of both technology and management practice is a reality. Response to such rapid-paced transformations requires a dramatic shift from the CEOs and the top and senior managers. The shift has to emerge in maps and definitions held by employees of organizations, its structures, tasks, relationships, role-taking processes and interfaces in formal and functional work settings.

Similarly, the Indian organizations have grown by the competency and capabilities of these very same people. India as a country has grown into the seventh-largest and now third-largest industrialized nation by the very same industrialists and by the very same employees and industries. Given the reality that this was not enough, sufficient or adequate does not overnight make a whole nation of people or employees in organizations redundant in their experience, knowledge, capability and competency. Organizations do not become obsolete in all their technology, existing structures and systems, management practices, leadership styles and managerial orientations. There existed a work culture, a work ethos, relationship processes, authority and hierarchy, interfaces and boundaries in Indian organizations which made Indian organizations grow. The impact of IT boom has confronted many of these practices and rightly so new dilemmas of growth are a reality and they need to be addressed, however.

In many organizations when all such events of social-emotional associations have been delinked from living practices of the organization the dysfunctionality and interface tensions have increased across levels in the organizations. This has happened more so when the owner-managers, entrepreneurs and CEOs have disassociated from these interfaces and moved on to business initiatives and new choices.

Let us look at how the Indian organizations grew in the traditional business context of India and what maps and definitions of people and systems they brought to the organizations when they joined these organizations.

After the turbulent seventies and formal consolidation of the eighties, the Indian organizations began transforming the organization culture. This transformation was through the introduction of new technology, into formally designed organization structures and a professional managerial and employee orientation. Most of the Indian organizations had truly panicked in the nineties when the Indian economy opened and there was an influx of industry and organizations across the world.

The Indian organizations' internal unpreparedness and the external giant image of global organizations created in the leadership and the employees of Indian organization doubts about their own strengths and resources. Their entry and potential momentum of entry caused the fear of the mammoth and global MNCs and the ruthlessness of the MNCs in destroying and swallowing the small businesses as well as existing Indian businesses. The quick selling of the Thumbs Up brand fanned more such fears. These apprehensions of the changing environment rekindled centuries-old doubts and evaluations of the capabilities and competencies of Indian strengths. A comparative frame enveloped by ethnic prejudices and labeling Indians as natives governed the assessment of India's reality. These comparative frames did not acknowledge the history of a millennium of brutalization, humiliation, exploitation and destruction of dignity and intellectual capabilities of millions in the nation. They did not perceive and consider the millennium of comparative and aggressive frames of reference which governed India. They also did not recognize the present six decades of autonomy and freedom in which the Indian organizations have grown and encountered the shifting sands of time. The Indian organizations have grown from small to medium to large to mammoth and global. A country with such complexity and diversity of race, religion, color and gender which has consolidated its industrialization and arrived at this crossroad to be considered an emerging power nation is to be commended rather than given itself critical and harsh judgments. As it stands today, the Indian organizations and employees have the internal capacity to evolve new perspectives on vision, strategies of growth of management structures, systems and processes to respond to opportunities and challenges of tomorrows' business environment.

All that the employees across levels require is to receive management education, tools and techniques and inspiration from the top leadership and a learning growing environment to take the destiny of the organization forward. Figure 3 presents the growth processes of Indian organizations.

Figure 3: Growth of Indian Organizations

i. The past of Indian organizations consists of various cycles of growth from inception, consolidation and further growth, plateauing and further growth with traditional management practices of the leadership.

ii. The present is a new threshold whereby the choice of transformation has occurred through new technology and organization structure, systems and processes.

iii. The future is where global opportunities and challenges beckon the organization.

{Parikh, Indira .J, Organization Cultural Transformation Process, A Study of Mahindra & Mahindra Tractor Division, Indian Institute of Management (Ahmedabad), (Jan – May 1997)}

The Indian organizations have gone through several phases of growth and consolidation through traditional management where people were many, the pace of work was slow and the product sold was in the seller's market place. Then came phase-2 where the traditional attitudes, orientations required change through investment in people through management learning and training in management practices and changes by adding new dimensions to managerial roles. The emphasis was on modernization, new technology and new global challenges. In this transformation, leaders played a critical and significant role as they mobilized a large number of employees through inspiration and educating them into new definitions of managerial roles. They also redefined management and corporate governance.

In this flux and transition, the people-factor, the human resource factor viz. the employees of the organization were squarely caught between the historical organizational and socio-cultural processes of personalized relationships with the leaders. They confronted the new and different assumptions of technology and work cultures and the assumptions of the formal, functional and professional management structures, systems and processes. All of a sudden the Indian organizations were seen to be filled with mediocre and non-productive employees; the organization was lacking a work culture, and professionalism and work ethics. A whole lot of similar other evaluations and judgments about a large number of Indian organizations as well as a very large number of its people began to surface. What seemed to have happened was that to the mass of employees logically and rationally the borrowed technology and management structures were acceptable. What was not acceptable were the role models and leadership and authority relationship anchored in formal functional processes. Both were necessary for transition and growth. However, the polarization of traditional versus professional created enormous stress both in the organizations as well as employees.

When the leaders of the organizations responded to the growth and the new challenges and opportunities, they got preoccupied largely with the growth of the organizations and created distance between the employees and the top leadership. The employees experienced dissonance and loss of personal contact. This was perceived as a loss of interest and involvement in that unit, division, organization and as well as the people. The employees often felt lost and orphaned. This then contributed to inefficiency, lethargy, invisible wastage of resources, loss of emotional contact and direction from the leader and a feeling of being disowned by the leaders. This further created ambivalence toward developmental focus, direction for change and growth. Not that the employees were left directionless; competent and capable heads of organizations came were sentence to the employees but in many organizations the employees especially the workers, staff and superiors found it difficult to accept the transition.

When an organization grows in size and turnover, it may be because of the business opportunities in the external national, regional and global opportunities. The organization may have invested in BPR-Business Process Reengineering and/or acquired state-of-the-art technology for further growth. The people in the organization also grow with the organization. However, after a point of time in some situations, the organization may continue to grow by the pull of opportunities in the environment but the people in the organization often remain frozen in their roles or in the earlier and old ways of working. Work performance with reference to the demands of the organization deteriorates and people get rooted in their job specialization and older techniques and skills. Many do not acquire an organizational or systemic perspective nor do they want to respond to the newer opportunities available to them. Some organizations become aware of this frozenness of the people in the organization and initiate steps to bring new energy into the people and the organization. Very often, there may be nothing seriously wrong with the organization or with the employees but there is a nagging belief among the key role-holders, HR and leadership that something is missing. There is no way to identify or pinpoint what is missing or what is wrong. There is an overall awareness of loss, a lull, a restlessness, which generates anxiety, apprehension and a need for action.

It is in such a context and situation that the HR with the support from the leadership and top management decides on an intervention that is comprehensive and holistic. It is in such times that an OD intervention is called for to facilitate the renewal and regeneration of both employees and the organizations.

OD Intervention

This book is all about transformations. The story began when the country was in the upheaval of 'change'. 'Change' was all about organizations craving for opportunities to grow, challenges to cope with the opening up of the economy, trying to run the race when they have felt tied down, entering an environment wished for but able to enter and trying to swim against the flow. 'Change' was a buzz word, changing economies both national and global was an experienced reality and all that was known and familiar seemed to be outdated and obsolete. Organizations and managers grappled with the transformations required in the employees across levels to respond to the changing business landscape of the organizations and to help them acquire skills and role orientations that would strengthen the organizations to run the race.

It is in this context and backdrop of changing national scenarios that organizations initiated and attempted Organization Development and Design Developmental inputs to facilitate managerial responses to the changing business scenarios. Generally, organizations have developmental or training inputs for a few of the managers who are sent out to the training programs which are perceived and experienced as either a punishment to leave their jobs to go and travel for such programs or as a reward to go to a good institution or good hotels to enjoy and learn something. Some, of course, experienced the training programs as a time to invest in themselves for growth and prepare themselves with knowledge, attitudes and skills for future positions and/or change of designation or positional responsibilities.

This was also a time when the focus of training and development was shifting to learning and development. New frameworks of learning were emerging to respond to the requirements of the organizations as well as managers to take newer and larger roles as the process of expansion and growth were accelerating at a pace not known before. The learning and development focus also brought out a more holistic emphasis on preparing employees across levels of the organizations. It was no more the top and senior people going to be prepared but employees across the organization were required to prepare themselves for the dramatic technological innovations which were beginning to make their appearance. These innovations would change lifestyles and ways of working the glimpses of which were beginning to be felt across the country and globally.

Such OD interventions became the need of the hour in the seventies and eighties in India. OD consultants came from the behavioral science streams, came from management sciences streams, came from policy strategy streams and responded to the calls of the organizations. Many Indian professors of management institutions of repute did OD work which transformed many organizations.

Organizations were moving from small scale and medium enterprises to large, mammoth and global organizations. Indian organizations were entering partnerships, alliances, strategic alliances, mergers and acquisitions and public-private partnerships. The mobility of employees was happening at a dizzying pace. New industries were beginning to appear on the business landscape of the country. New names in leadership roles were beginning to reverberate on the Indian organizational scenario. And a whole new concept of managers and managerial roles were beginning to be sought after in the world of organizations.

It is at such a configuration of the evolution of Indian business environment, Indian industry, Indian organizations, employees of Indian organizations, that the introduction of newer technologies, IT revolution and the whole of mobiles, laptops, Facebook, Twitter, I-pods, I-pads and similar other inventions appeared. The other dimensions of the configuration are the malls, retail environment of branded and other goods and the multicultural cuisine available both in rural and urban India. All these create a unique juxtaposition where people in general and employees of work organizations need to transform themselves to respond and integrate with the emerging reality of India.

It is in this kaleidoscope of Indian landscape that many organizations in the late eighties and nineties realized the need for a holistic approach to investing in their managers. Parikh's work with Indian organizations and Indian managers and the transformations occurring in Indian organizations became a starting point to study the whole organization and to explore the possibilities of what were the hurting spots in the organization and why. The people in the organizations had brought the organizations this far and most had done well given the context in which they were operating. Now was the time for propelling the organization to a different level of growth and with the people they had or bring in additional people through recruitment and slowly but certainly start transforming the existing organization work culture. It was time to move forward, it was time for transforming employees to help them discover their potentials and to translate organizational potentials to a growth path and to success and excellence. The time for Indian organizations had come to crystallize their work identity and to emerge as contributing to the growth of the economy.In understanding the historical evolution and growth, many organizations went through similar patterns of growth. As in the fifties and sixties, the Indian business environment was also similar; the patterns also were similar in general but had specific characteristics in particular. Moreover, each organization needed to be understood in their respective business context, the individuals as leaders who governed the organization, the focus of management, and the people who joined, when they joined, at which phase of growth they joined and the level within the organization structure they joined. The interplay of all these elements created a unique dynamics of the organization's way of working, the work ethos and its work culture which contributed to the writing of the organization history and the organization story.

The organization story and the history of growth can be categorized in each of the decades beginning sixties. Each decade converged in the pace of growth, focus of growth, the leadership roles and the people who entered the organization. The next sets of statements reflect the evolution of four decades of organization transformation.

The Decade of the Sixties

The sixties was a time of the business environment settling down. It was just about a decade and more of India taking the steps to industrialization and self-governance. The idealism was still around, the euphoria of independence was just settling down and the industries were beginning to emerge and struggle to grow under economic and government policies and regulations. The organizations were partly settling down with their partly designed and partly evolved structure internally. For the employees who entered the organizations, this was their first job. Out of institutions of higher education, they were happy to be in a job when the land was of scarcity, and some joined because it was a job and not the preferred choice or passion of many. The decade the employees worked within the organization encountered some of the transformations and critical events that many carried as organization history and their personal memory.

As the transformations begin to occur and the organization starts to move forward, some elements of formalization begin to appear. The past then acquires a nostalgic image of the organization and its people with whom the employees interacted with. This was more so with the seniors and colleagues. During the initial years, being a project phase of the organization and the setting up of the organization, the employees brought a lot of enthusiasm and excitement of contribution. The young employees were full of dreams and aspirations and were looking forward to a long association and careers with the organizations. Many of the young entrants were the first-generation graduates and postgraduates and engineers.

The structure though designed was informal, and the inter-phases were more direct and personal rather than structural and hierarchical. When new initiatives were taken all celebrated with happiness and there was an air of festivity in the organizations as the beginning created memories of togetherness and being part of the team and groups to build an organization. The leadership roles were available to the employees and many of them addressed them often to encourage and mobilize them for productivity and efficiency. Most employees felt that the organization was their second home, seniors their parents or uncles and the relationships were largely anchored in the social structures and role-related behavior. The authority was to be respected and obeyed and the work needed to be completed, no matter how long it took. The employees across levels accepted the organization as their own and worked toward a common cause. They accepted the responsibility and the concept of duty and appropriate role behavior.

The sixties as a decade seemed to be the best decade before the organizations, the supervisors and workers were transformed into a behavior pattern which became very difficult for the managers of the seventies. To some of the managers, authority and hierarchy worked as it should have, the discipline of time and punctuality could be maintained without much difficulty, and the unions were collaborative. All this and many other carry-over behaviors from the social system facilitated the work culture to be cohesive and conducive to the emergence of a work culture suited for the times.

The Decade of the Seventies

The seventies saw significant and critical transformations in the industrial sector of the country. By this time the organizations had grown by the very pull of the external business environment. The land of scarcity was pulling the organizations to respond to the challenges and opportunities. The organization had to recruit more people and in larger numbers, the existing employees were being promoted, and the demands for the salaries were increasing. The organization structure needed to be redesigned as the organization was growing, the geographical boundaries were expanding which started to demand a corporate structure and the need was felt to work with consultants who could help the organization with planning and strategizing growth. The growth in size created a need for formalization and setting up of systems to manage the people-part of the organizations. The combination and interplay of all these dynamics which were not formally addressed started to create dysfunctional patterns of behavior in the organization.

The seventies also confronted the organization with management and union issues. The sixties were the time when it seemed the government was supportive of the unions for their causes of social welfare. However, at the same time, the issues of productivity and quality were ignored. Over the decade the fragmentation and polarization between the management and the unions began to grow at a rapid pace. By the time seventies came around, the distances had grown very large and the focus on the organization as well as the growth of the country was completely forgotten. The environments, both internal and external, were in turmoil. In this turmoil both the performance of employees and the productivity slowed down; the markets were also beginning to shift from being a sellers' market to buyers' market. The focus became so inward for their own protection that the organization was quite lost. The dynamics between the management and the union impacted the roles of the managers across levels and slowly but steadily, the managers began to disengage from asserting and ensuring the work from the employees and especially the employees at the shop floor level. This resulted in entrenched interfaces across levels of the organization. Inter-functional linkages that were personalized and friendly began to decline. There was much aloofness and withholding began to emerge. Functional boundaries began to be tightly held. Walls across roles and functions began to be built and they were higher and higher and were protected by the role-holders.

In the seventies, as the organization started to experience the stabilization of management education and outpouring of professionally educated young men and women, the organizations in their attempts to grow began to recruit these young entrants, engineers and fresh graduates and postgraduates. This created a pattern of interfaces in the organizations. The people's profile began to change and the culture of the organization began to transform. There were polarization and fragmentation across the profiles of people. The people with a long history and newly recruited people spoke a different language, had different ambitions, values and expectations from the organizations. The people with long association and history started to feel excluded and undervalued by the very same people with whom they had started to work. This created much angst in them. However, the newer recruits pushed the frontiers of the organization in terms of wages, benefits and supportive infrastructures.

Moreover, the definition, meaning and the role maps of employees were deeply influenced by the social system and the interfaces across levels of the organization continued to be impacted by the social structures of the family and society. This was evident in the workshops where the objectives were to redesign interfaces in the context of formal work organizations.

The Decade of the Eighties

The decade of the eighties heralded a major transformation in the economic policies of the government, the opening up of the economy, the internationalization and globalization of the country. The country was beginning to open up its windows to the world outside and to some extent open its doors so that the people inside could see and step outside and outside people enter inside. This opening created another set of turbulences and simultaneously created fears, anxieties, apprehensions on thereon hand and hoes, ambitions and aspirations to take the organizations to new thresholds and horizons of growth. The impact of technology, the young generation becoming vocal, the impact of the IT industry and the emerging mobility of employees—for the first time, the nation was beginning to experience the impact of the intellectual evolution of Indians.

The organizations now had employees of four generations reflecting unique configuration of values, beliefs, traditions, education, expectations and ambitions. One set was anchored in the traditional Indian society and the emerging set was anchored in the post-independence modern society of India influenced by the west, mostly the North American as different from the influences of the UK.

The turbulent seventies had brought spurts in growth and constant turmoil. The eighties brought the focus on consolidation of growth through the formalization of organizations. This happened through redesigning organization structures, designing systems and management processes. The growth of the organization in size, turnover and multiple products were beginning to make their impact felt on the employees. The role holder was experiencing the pressure to interface more for tasks and not with enduring social associations or history of working together. Task competences were becoming more visible and sought after. Departments, functions, divisions and across geographical locations there were pulls and pushes of each one's significance, contribution and importance. The hierarchy was acquiring criticality in terms of power, significance and dominance.

In this process of growth, the people-factor was acquiring immense significance. The growth made it necessary that the organizations compete in the market place in quality and excellence as well as in terms of turnover. This made it necessary that people be equipped in knowledge, skills, attitudes and behavior as well as the perspectives of both the external and external environment. At the interface level, though the intensities of entrenchments, intolerance and inflexibility of management and union had settled down, the overall mistrust, suspicions, and distance between the management and the union had increased. These differences started to appear across the different levels and sectors of the organization. Each level and sector created their own little islands and started to get isolated. The interfaces began to fray and distances started to increase.

It was at this point of time that the organizations began to recognize the need for investing in people and transforming the existing culture of the organization to a work culture that would challenge itself for growth and movement forward. The organization needed to realign itself to the opportunities of the present as well as anticipate the need of the future. Around this time (the eighties) the management education had acquired significance and immense criticality. The graduates from management institutions were being sought after and considered assets as they were employment-ready and could propel the organization forward. Similarly, OD and ODD as well as organization consultants were accepted as the source and resource for the organization to transform the work culture and take the organization to walk the new paths.

The Decade of the Nineties

The decade of the nineties transformed the country. From being a country of scarcity the country started to witness its first signs of prosperity for larger groups of people. From very large families there was a distinct shift to smaller families. The joint family structure was transforming into smaller and nuclear families. The parents working were a reality. The children who grew up in such homes were the new-age children who lived life differently and the parents were also the first or the second-generation free Indians.

The liberalization, globalization and opening up of the economy confronted the Indian organizations with unprecedented challenges and opportunities for growth. Organizations had to respond with choices of restructuring, choices of new technology, upgrading the knowledge, attitudes and skills and professionalizing the management as well as the organization.

When new choices were made, when the leadership identified new directions for the organization and new technologies were introduced, the leadership believed that the employees would follow and respond with the same clarity as they had. However, there was a vast distance between what was introduced and how the employees could respond to it. Very often a response lag started to occur between the pace of transformations initiated and the pace of responses that came. The employees could not keep pace with the expectations as well as the demands of the organizations.

The organizations were growing in size and the structures were being designed from departmental, functional, and divisional to SBU structures. Any restructuring requires the relocation of employees and movement from one level to another. Designations change, authority and power are redistributed, and some acquire better positioning while others do not. This creates and leaves residues and baggage in the employees. This happens more so to the existing employees who have been associated with the organizations for a very long time. This is experienced very vividly when new employees join the organization with better wages and possibilities and for each of this restructuring, the employees required inputs and training to respond with appropriate work profiles. The employees required clarity of jobs, tasks, roles and performance. Moreover, they required clarity of functional and role linkages so that the input-output-input model could work effectively.

Around this time and phase of transformation in the economy and the thrust of the government toward growth, the powers of the unions were being weakened as the market conditions were more on competition, quality, excellence and volume. All the equations and power dynamics of the management-union interface got anchored in the survival of the organization rather than who should be in power and control. The government also recognized the need for freedom of the industries to grow to compete in the global market place. As such, there was a slow but certain shift in the equation between management and the unions. The very same unions who would fight the management when they introduced new technology and argued against the loss of jobs now recognized that if the organizations did not opt for reengineering or the state-of-the-art technology, the organizations had no possibility of survival, and that would definitely be harmful and disastrous for the large segment of the employees. As such, there was just the emergence of a shared understanding between the management and the unions.

This understanding made it possible for the organization to redesign organization structures, systems of the individual, team and organizational appraisal, and introduce management processes to upgrade and professionalize the organization.

The Turn of the Century

The turn of the century created dramatic shifts in the mindsets of the country. There was a sudden breakthrough in the structure of economic growth in the country which started slowly but steadily in the eighties. The IT sector mushroomed from nowhere and everywhere like magic. With it came the breakthrough in the acceptance of technology by the masses. Beginning with pagers, to setting up of PCU and ISD, television from one set in building to many to all homes, to television in each room, and then the mobiles for exclusivity, to the mobiles in every pocket, computers, I-pads and I-phones and the subsequent revolution, the Indian masses began to transform. The most ancient country was becoming younger day-by-day and the revolution of growth was intensifying its pace.

Organizations were beginning to look outward for opportunities; the country was beginning to feel small, and an India which could not have dreamed that it would become an MNC across other countries. This phenomenon created an avalanche-effect of a country whose basic character had begun to change. Yet there were many aspects where the country continued to remain the same and many aspects where the country began to dramatically transform.

And amidst all this, once again the organizations realized that though there were many employees who were responding to change at the pace required by the organization, there were still a larger number of employees who were caught in their comfort zone and needed to be directed to the new destinations of their career growth and as well as the growth of the organization. This required the organizations and a large segment of the employees to a wakeup call from their slumber to a reality that had never existed before. In these two decades, some of the organizations had lost one or two waves of phenomenal growth, while some other organizations could ride the waves of growth high and mighty and made their impact across the world.

Slowly, the ivory towers crumbled, and the islands of isolation acquired mobility to move and the shape of new organizations began to emerge. Each individual, group and organization were confronted with new opportunities and challenges as well as demands to perform in the emerging global economy. In the new organizational structure, responsibilities and accountability increased, authority was of the role and not the hierarchy and seniority, and the individuals were expected to align themselves to the vision as well as enlarge their horizons. A new and wider managerial role anchored in a broader organizational perspective was necessary across all levels of the organization.

The shift also made it necessary that the employees across levels respond to effective inter-functional linkages, teamwork, understand task interdependencies, and planning and strategizing for growth. Indian organizations stood at both the threshold and crossroads, and it was up to the leadership to choose the directions, destinations and prepare its people to walk and perhaps run the chosen path.

The organizations were ready to provide learning and developmental inputs across the layers of the organizations so that when it came for a sprint, or a dash or a marathon the employees would be ready. It is in this context that Parikh was invited to design many learning and developmental modules in some of the organizations to begin the creation of pathways of learning where a large number of employees would walk.

This book explores through storytelling methodology and the analysis of the stories as well as their interpretations, the process of transformation initiated by some organizations through a holistic approach of learning and development of their employees across three levels: junior, middle and senior-level of management. The organizations were all concerned with growth, expansion, the introduction of new technology and people who were in the organization for decades. Most of the employees did not have experience of other organizations, nor had they the exposure required to perceive the kind of transformations that were occurring and required of their roles. They were men or women devoted to their jobs, they knew the job they had done for long and were confused and perplexed at the changes occurring in the external environment. Their aspirations were rising, their need to move forward was increasing, their willingness to propel the organization forward was high and their aspiration to be part of the new environment was immense. However, what the organization's growth and the new challenges and opportunities required of their roles were not clear to them.

It was important at this stage to assess the level of awareness and the level of clarity that existed in the managers across levels. The organizations in which Parikh (1996 onwards) was invited wanted her to study and assess the whole organization and assess the employees so that relevant inputs of learning and development could be designed for them. The approach was to do an internal benchmarking study of the organization and to align the employees with the directions of growth the organization was visualizing. It was also to assess the employees their present understanding and then to design the necessary inputs.

It is with this perspective that Parikh identified a methodology of TAT (Thematic Apperception Test) which uses pictures of people and situations of different settings. Here the participants write stories in response to the situations on the cards. We use seven cards depicting:

- One-person situation
- Two-people situation and
- Group situation

Based on the data collected and the workshops conducted as part of the organization assignment this book has been written.

There are five chapters to this book.

1. History of growth of Indian Organization
2. Storytelling as a methodology of learning and development
3. Stories by managers
4. Findings & Conclusion from the Stories: What do the stories tell?
5. Organizational Maturity Perspective for Tomorrow

SYNOPSIS OF CHAPTER 2 - STORYTELLING AS A METHODOLOGY OF LEARNING AND DEVELOPMENT

With the rapid innovations in technology, organizations recognized the need for upgrading the knowledge, attitudes and multiple skills of their employees required to respond to the changes occurring both in the external and internal environment. A whole stream of new content methodologies, pedagogy and perspectives began to emerge and the process of learning through a projective methodology provided the possibilities of exploration of maps and definitions of roles and the organization as held by individual, collectivity and the organization itself.

The authors have extensively used the Thematic Apperception Test (TAT), a projective personality test consisting of 31 pictures depicting various situations, settings and people. They selected seven cards. Though the TAT situations are used for many purposes, the authors found TAT situations to be a very effective tool to explore the maps and definitions of work roles as held by employees across levels of the organization. The meanings they gave to the internal and external business environment, their perception of relationships across levels and roadblocks and the experience of the landscape of the work organization. The content and process analysis and interpretations further facilitate the understanding of the roles played by the organizations as well as the continuous influences of the socio-cultural and familial context (primary system). The context of the stories also brought to surface the impact of formal educational institutions, work organizations and the external environment. The focus of understanding and exploring these dimensions was on undoing the knots as held by the employees and creating an internal space for new roles and initiatives to begin.

In this chapter, the authors have used the TAT stories to connect to the organizational context, the meaning and definition held by individuals of the context, their own roles taken in the organization, their interface with the seniors in the hierarchy and authority, and their interface with subordinates and peers. The authors have documented examples of simple to complex stories.

CHAPTER 2

STORYTELLING AS A METHODOLOGY OF LEARNING AND DEVELOPMENT

Introduction:

Organizations need to transform from one state of existence, growth, performance, productivity and responsiveness to the competition, opportunities and challenges of the environment to a different state of growth, unfolding, wellbeing of people to property and generation of wealth. The business of the organization can grow by the pulls of the external environment and demands from the internal environment viz. people. The state-of-the-art infrastructures can be created given the availability of resources and the existing and potential infrastructures available in the country. The state-of-the-art technology can be available again given the resources and needs of the organizations to upgrade themselves or for the growth of the organization. However, for any of this growth to happen and to be initiated and implemented the people-part of the organization requires innovative responses, creativity and mobilizing the people across levels to respond to the opportunities and challenges. Given the transformations occurring globally as well as the external and internal environment of the organization and as well as business and industry, the learning and growth inputs to upgrade and professionalism, the organization and its employees come out as one of the key thresholds the organization needs to cross.

With the beginning of industrialization and introduction of technology across the decades, organizations have recognized the need for first upgrading the knowledge, attitudes and skills and second to help them acquire perspectives and broader horizon maps of their employees from time to time so that they keep pace with the growth as well as the fast-paced transformations.

Organizations have designed, adopted, adapted and responded to the needs of the organization's growth and the need of the employees to grow in their careers, knowledge, responsiveness and the multiple skill sets required to engage with the changes occurring. The innovation in technology has created an avalanche-effect of transforming the organization's environment. New paths have had to be created or found to respond. History of organization and HR have come up with the development of tools and techniques to help employees become aware and assess their abilities and competencies as well as the growth they need to initiate and shape themselves into.

With the rapid innovations in technology a whole stream of new content methodologies, pedagogy and perspectives began to emerge. Organization, HR and OD consultants beginning with the earlier giants like Prof. Dharni P. Sinha, Gouranga Chattopadhyay, Udai Pareek, Pulin K. Garg, Dr. B.L Maheshwari and many others responded to this call and developed education modules. The next generation Prof. T V Rao, Somnath Chattopadhyay and many others first followed their footsteps and then began designing management modules based on the relevance of the times of the organizations' growth and changing economic problems and scenario.

Beginning mid-seventies Parikh has used several perspectives on learning and development methodologies benchmarking the present status of the competencies for both organization and individuals and then developing learning modules to upgrade knowledge and evolve relevant perspectives.

The introduction of projective tools of assessment and use of their methodology is an ancient process. The practice of psychology and psychotherapy began with Freud and was followed by many others; this methodology has been used for assessment for both individual and organization assessment. Beginning with the dreams and their interpretations of premonitions, the use of art, drawings and stories, metaphors and folklore, folktales and myths, symbols and symbolisms and many others are various manifestations of projections of individuals and groups. These are to understand individual role maps and definitions, experiences and observations, meanings and interpretations which shape their roles both in the primary system which is the family and society culture and secondary system which is the educational institutions, work organizations and the external environment. The projections also facilitate identifying the role stances, then the feeling and emotional tonality and then identity of the individual collectivity and the organization. These influence the secondary system organization and the work organizations shape the evolving of a work ethos and a work culture of the organization. Put together, all these influences shape the identity of the individuals collectively and the organization.

Parikh in her role as a consultant to many organizations has first conducted an internal benchmarking study to assess the organization through exploring and understanding the history of growth: the past and present work ethos and work culture of the individual and multiple leadership role models operating in the organization, and how the employees have performed their roles in the past and are performing in the present to arrive at the learning and development needs of the employees.

Once this is arrived at, a choice of methodology is made and accordingly the inputs are designed. Parikh has found that to start the process of learning, a projective methodology provides an entry into maps and definitions of roles as held by individuals and collectivities. Parikh has extensively used the Thematic Apperception Test as a very effective projective methodology to explore the maps and definitions of work roles as held by employees across levels of the organization, their internal and external business orientations, their perception of roadblocks and barriers (both internal and external) and the very definition of their experience of the landscape of the work organization. The content and process analysis and interpretations further facilitate the understanding of roles played by the organizations as well as the continuous influences of the socio-cultural and familial context {primary system}. It also facilitates the understanding of and the impact of formal educational institutions, work organizations and the external environment. The focus of understanding and exploring these dimensions are first to loosen and then undo the knots and finally create an internal space for new roles to emerge and initiatives to begin.

The TAT is a projective personality test that was designed at Harvard in the 1930s by Christiana D. Morgan and Henry A. Murray. The TAT is one of the most widely used psychological tests across ages and for a whole spectrum of understanding individuals' group and organizational behavior. A projective test is one in which a person's patterns of thought, attitudes, observational capacity, and emotional responses are evaluated on the basis of responses to ambiguous test materials. The TAT consists of 31 pictures that depict a variety of social and interpersonal situations. The subject is asked to tell or write a story about each picture to the examiner. These stories are then analyzed and interpreted based on the purpose for which the stories were asked to be written. Our purpose to use the TAT methodology was to help the participants in the program who were the employees of an organization to understand their own roles past and present, identify the internal and external barriers which they perceived and to release energy for them to come up with meaningful responses in their work roles. As such, out of these 30 cards, the author selected seven cards depicting seven different settings of the organizations which had unique themes and across the life-space which reflected multiple and various roles. These cards were specific to represent the context of an organization and their interpersonal dynamics in an organization.

Objectives of TAT in OD Intervention

1. To understand and facilitate work roles through clarity of job, function, task and role performed by self and others,

2. To understand the boundary conditions across functions, roles and inter-linkages required for role interface and teamwork,

3. To explore the intricacies of relationship across the hierarchy, authority and levels of management in the given structure and the framework of the organization,

4. To understand nature and meaning of achievement, success and failure of self, others and the system and to discover abilities to cope and manage both,

5. To be able to work as a group for managerial and organization growth, excellence and effectiveness.

In other words, TAT can be used to examine and assess the *soft skills* of employees i.e. personality traits, personal habits, friendliness, levels of motivation, optimism and achievement and interpersonal skills, etc. Such people and social skills complement the *hard skills* e.g. dealing with technology and machines; the technical requirements of a job (in the case of organizations in Information Technology employees need to be adept in software programming, operations, etc.) are on the one hand dealing with the client and their own teams on the other hand.

Soft skills are not a replacement of hard skills—they are most often complementary and necessary so that the human face of the individual is not lost behind machines and/or isolation. Studies conducted by many Psychologists reveal such skills, contribute to an employee's ability to motivate and challenge himself/herself, helps the employee to be self-aware of his/her limitations and strengths, etc. and ultimately helps the employee to discover his/her potential, thus benefiting the individual as well as the organization.

Test Applications

Thematic Apperception Test is used to measure the following:

i. Individual potentials at induction/entry levels, be it their first job or at senior levels of the organization,

ii.   Recruitment/Selection to identify the integration and openness to adapt to the exciting work culture of the organization,

iii. Identifying the focus of training needs so that the individual and the organizations are aligned,

iv.   Designing a career path at a pace in which the individual is comfortable,

v.   Succession planning,

vi.   Promotions and the focus of developmental inputs tried to the new roles and responsibilities,

vii. Performance Appraisal and educational inputs so that the employees have a benchmark of how they are playing their role,

viii. Leadership role and potentials,

ix.   Cultural fit with the organization and where they can contribute and make a difference, and

x.   Individual directions for career and choices in life as well as membership in multiple systems and multiple roles.

Description and Meaning of the Cards

In the first module of L & D Parikh chose the following seven cards depicting seven different situations, ages, phases of career growth in the context of the organization

Card I

(Adapted from TAT test cards)

Description: This card shows a young man sitting at a work desk. There is a photograph frame of a woman and children. There is a window facing him.

Meaning: This card brings out the attitudes to job, meaning of work, achievement, aspirations, ambitions, social relationships, family, multiple roles and the themes around self-motivation, involvement and commitment.

Card 2

(Adapted from TAT test cards)

Description: This card shows an old man and a young man in an interaction, both dressed formally in either an office or a formal setting. There is a photograph/painting of a formally dressed older man on a wall.

Meaning: This card brings out the relationship theme across generations or across hierarchy. The emerging themes are around father-son and/ or superior-subordinate. Occasionally the younger man is the boss and the older man the loyal subordinate of the father. The themes are around authority, power, control, loyalty, conformity, and change in expectations, autonomy and independence.

Card 3

(Adapted from TAT test cards)

Description: This card shows a group of men in different postures around a table.

Meaning: The theme is around groups, teams and colleagues either in a formal meeting or an informal friendly social setting. The theme revolves around achievement, results, and interpersonal relationships, in the context of either teamwork or social informal gathering.

Card 4

(Adapted from TAT test cards)

Description: This card shows a scarcely clad young man on a rope.

Meaning: The theme is around achievements, success, fulfillment, and aspirations and reflects whether the individual sees himself ascending or descending the rope. The card is symbolic or the person's faith in himself and his abilities.

Card 5

(Adapted from TAT test cards)

Description: This card shows a well-dressed middle-aged man sitting on a chair by a window with a book and glasses on his lap.

Meaning: The theme is around success, achievement, accomplishment and reflecting and reviewing on past, present or future. The theme portrays success and satisfaction.

Card 6

(Adapted from TAT test cards)

Description: This card shows a rural setting with a casually dressed young man sitting on a fence talking to an older man dressed in a suit.

Meaning: The theme is around an encounter between a stranger and a known person who belong to two different contexts—rural and urban. The interaction is about belonging, values, beliefs and attitudes around relationships, interactions and authority. This card brings out the residual issues of Card 2 on relationships.

Card 7

(Adapted from TAT test cards)

Description: This card shows an elderly man sitting on a desk, which is full of files with a coat and a hat on a tray. The other desks are empty as well as no one is around.

Meaning: The theme is around success or failure, overwork and overengagement and meaning of work. The card is a counterpart to Card 5, which reflects success and relaxation. This card sometimes also portrays the continuity and residues of Card 1.

The cards are shown one at a time for 30 seconds. The participants are asked to observe the situation and people of each of the seven cards one at a time. A framework is given to structure their story. However, they are free to write on their own as they wish.

1. Activity going on

2. Who are the Characters

3. The interactions/interface between the characters within the situation which is happening

4. The outcome of the situation/people

The participants are then asked to write a story on what they see, who are the people they have identified and what is happening in the story. They are given 30 seconds to observe the situation and are given another five minutes to write their story; likewise, all seven cards are shown one at a time. Sometimes the seventh card is blank and the participants use their imagination to write the complete story. The stories on the seven cards are based on events with people or systems.

Parikh has used the stories to connect the written stories to the organization context, the meaning and definition held by individuals of the context, their own roles within the organization, and their interface with the seniors in the hierarchy and authority, their interface with subordinates and peers. The analyses and interpretation of the stories provide a glimpse of the individual's socio-psychological world reflecting both the primary and secondary systems.

The stories also provide the influences of the past roles in the present and the influences of the present which will impact their future roles. In this chapter, we deal with the managerial roles played out in the organization. The analysis of the stories first reflects the content of the story and the roles given to people where events and people are located in a context of social or work settings in which the individual plays their social or work roles. The content analyses of the stories reflect the maps and definitions of people and systems held by the participants of both the family and family members as well as the organization and work roles and social systems and social roles.

The stories are anchored both in family and work systems as well as society, culture, work organizations and the broader environment. However, often this is not so clearly stated but the context often may be embedded in the story but not written. Underlying the content analysis of the stories are embedded some basic assumptions and theoretical frameworks as well as the philosophy of work and life which the individuals live with. The content analysis, its explorations and interpretations provide the participants understanding, clarity and possibly freedom from obsolete and outgrown maps and definitions and find views relevant and meaningful role maps and definitions for both social and work settings.

1. **Socio-cultural context**: Any individual will be influenced and shaped by his/her experiences of growing up in the culture and society he/she is a part of. Individuals carry coding of norms and values heard by them through myths, epics, folklore and folktales. Individuals as part of growing up also internalize the roles of parents and other significant family members as they experience them in their relationships with them. The family plays an important and significant role in the growing up of the child. All these are his/her context and these emerge as continuity of the context of the individual. Whether the experience of the individual was at five or fifty, the psyche experiences it as similar or the same in the experience of the individual.

Once the participants have completed writing the stories some conceptual frameworks are offered to the participants to anchor their learning. The individual tends to locate the self in the center with the periphery of the area increasing depending upon where the individual is located. Figure 4 presents the models of those systems influencing the individual.

Figure 4: Forces Impacting the Individual

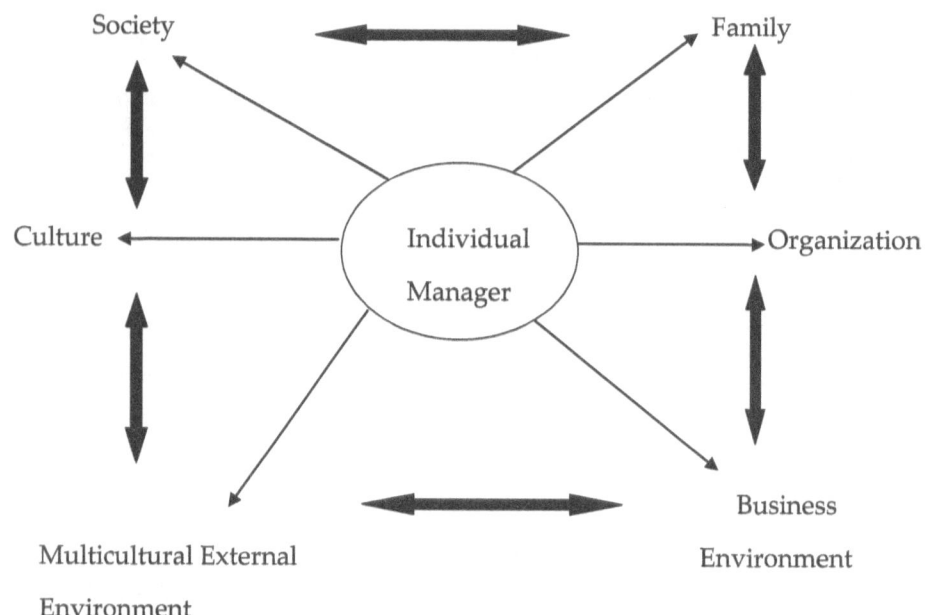

---

i. The individual is influenced and is located in the culture, society, family, external environment, business environment and the organization.

ii. The location and experience of space, on the one hand, impacts the behavior of the individual refugee.

iii. The individual's behavior in the role of a manager in an organization needs to be understood in terms of how much space he/she gives to himself/herself in any or all of these contexts.

{Adapted from Parikh, I.J. consultancy (Phase II, May. 1996), consultancy (Aug. 2003), consultancy (Aug. 2005), Parikh, I. J/Kollan. B (Aug. 2005), consultancy (July. 2007)}

All the above influence the individual shaping his role and how he/she configures the map and definition of social and work systems and social and work roles. The individual gives meaning and crystallizes his/her social and work roles and contributes to social and work culture as well as gives meaning to his identity. All these or some of the dimensions are reflected or not reflected in the story.

The relation/interdependence between the work and social culture has been a topic of interest to several researchers. Several research studies have looked at the activities of managers in the context of their whole lives, especially with regard to the work-family interface[1]. One set of studies examines the degree of conflict and tension in this interface. Such researchers believe that work and family demands are at all times incompatible and thus problematic and fraught with tension. This results in a negative spillover of thoughts, emotions, attitudes and behavior from one system to another.

Another set of studies has looked at the systems having a mutually benefiting interface. The multiple roles (in the work and family domain) result in a positive spillover of thoughts, emotions, attitudes, etc. Most studies, however, show a combination of both—positive and negative—perspectives. Based on the author's studies and workshops, it can be concluded that there is a continuous interplay between the primary and secondary systems and primary and secondary roles. Employees translate the emotive and cognitive maps and definitions of people and systems from both the primary and secondary systems into emotions and then take a stance vis-a-vis the people and systems at workplace.

The new configuration of the maps and definition of people and system as crystallized by the identity then determines both the social and work interfaces. The figure shown below reflects a framework to highlight how the individual can go beyond the primary and secondary and initiate an emergent map that is realistic and appropriate in the present and as such play meaningful roles. The individual's own recognition of the contribution of his personal identity on his role behavior then adds to the dynamic behavior in any system.

---

1   "Work-Family Interface experiences and coping strategies: Implications for entrepreneurship research and practice" Jennifer E Jennings. Megan S.McDougald. University of Alberta

Figure 5: Emergent Maps and Roles

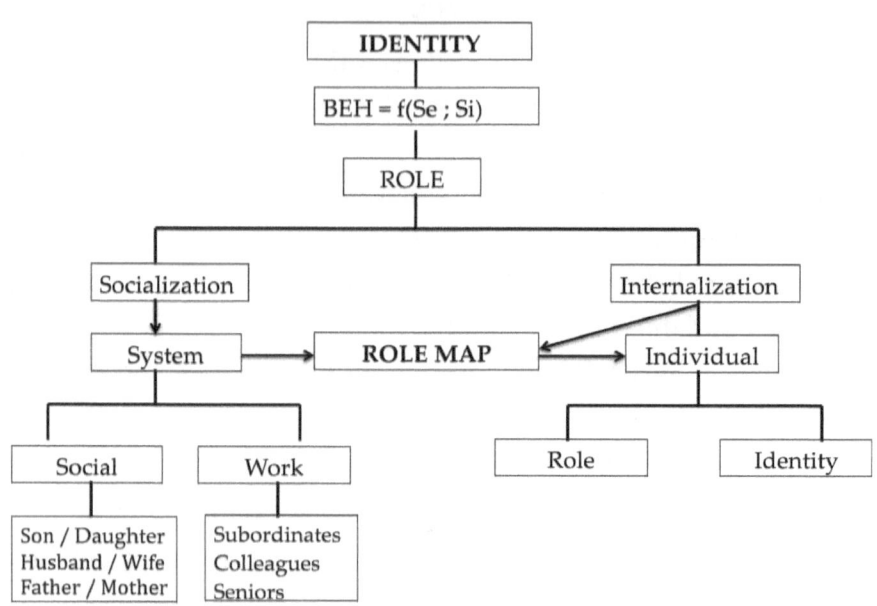

---

i. A human child is socialized for socially desirable roles.

ii. A human child internalizes both people and systems.

iii. Social roles are daughter/son, husband and wife and mother and father.

iv. Identity impacts roles and creates a unique configuration of role-taking.

{Adapted from Parikh, I.J. consultancy (Aug. 2005)}

Figure 6: Emotive Cognitive Role Maps and Definitions of People Systems

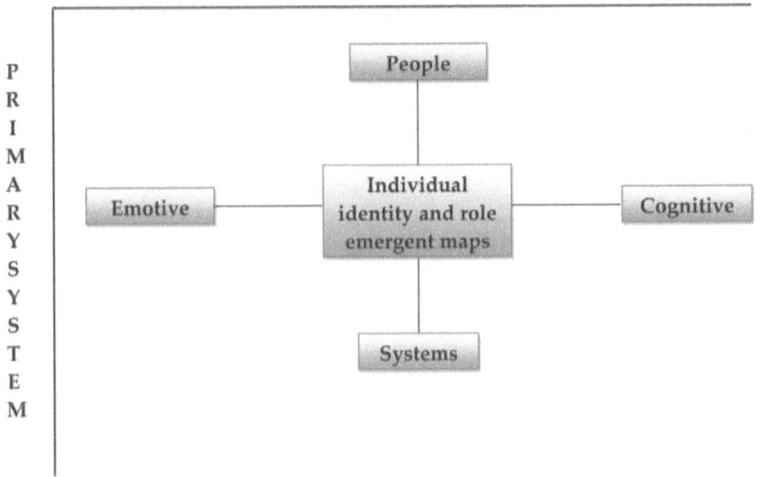

SECONDARY SYSTEM

i. An individual experiences the interplay of the primary system.

ii. An individual experiences the interplay of the secondary system.

iii. An individual experiences the pulls and pushes from the people of the primary system.

iv. An individual experiences the pulls and pushes from the people of the secondary system.

v. The individual finally arrives at a configuration of the emergent maps, which he adds to the emotive and cognitive processes of his identity. The emergent map is his unique personal map for role-taking.

{Adapted from Parikh, I.J. consultancy (Feb. 2002)}

Figure 7: Emotive Role Map of Primary & Secondary System

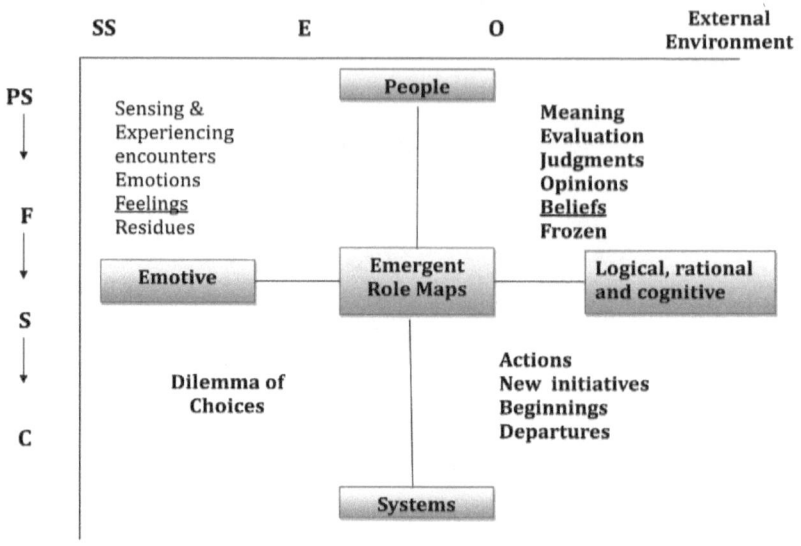

PS=Primary System, F=Family, S=Society, C=Culture
SS=Secondary System, E=Education institutions, O= Organization

i. There are two systems of Socialization Primary and Secondary systems

ii. Primary systems consist of family, society and cultures

iii. Secondary systems consist of education, work organization and external environment

iv. In the primary systems, individual experiences and encounters emotional sensitivity

v. In the work culture, individual acquires the logical, rational and cognitive meanings

vi. The emergent role is defined by the individual's own configuration of meanings to social and work-setting

vii. Growth means the dilemma of choices or

viii. In the work-setting, the individual is either subordinate, colleagues or superior

ix. The resolution of dilemmas are in action or initiatives and new beginnings

{Adapted from Parikh, I.J. consultancy (Aug. 2005)}

When the content analysis is explored with the participants from the stories it becomes clear that individuals may locate themselves in the primary system and/or in the secondary system. They may also strongly root themselves in one of the six systems. The dominant location then guides the individual to play his/her role accordingly.

When an individual is located in the culture, he/she tends to play out the idealistic role behavior and may not be open to the transformations in the role behavior of the present generation. He/she may tend to be critical, evaluative and judgmental. Similarly, if a younger generation is located in the present generation and culture, he/she may be critical, judgmental and evaluative of the older generation.

If the individual is located in the societal structures, norms and values of the society, his/her expectations of roles and behavior of himself and others will be role and rule-bound and may find it different to play his/her role in open and unstructured situations. He/she would tend to prefer strong boundary conditions and structured well-defined environment.

A person is located in the context of the family as the system which defines all behavior and appropriate code of conduct. Differences become creators of stress and there is a very strong right and wrong. Such individuals tend to largely talk about themselves and their systems of the past.

Individuals located in the education they have received or not received talk of their abilities, capabilities, competencies and their achievements and accomplishments.

Individuals located in the work organizations tend to derive a meaning from the organization and workplace and focus on the role and designations, power and positions and the authority they wield through controls.

Individuals located in the external environment have a lot of information, facts and figures sometimes from all sorts of sources.

Each of these locations is simultaneous in the individual and multiple at the same time. The configuration of the role emerges by the dominant influences and the meaning the individual has given to the experiences. However, a dominant pattern and a role emerge in the individual. The content analysis of the stories helps in the individual's understanding of his/her location and then discovering his/her own identity, his/her voice differentiating what belongs to him/her and what does not and then making choices or non-choices.

The content analysis and then interpretation provides exploration and discovery of differentiating primary system and secondary system and the primary role and the secondary role and finding the freedom to make meaningful, appropriate and relevant choices.

Very often in the context analysis and further interpretation to explore the identity of the individual and its impact on the role, initially, there is much reluctance and resistance to identify one's own contribution.

However, this is disowned and much of the constraints and difficulties are attributed to external sources. As such, the analysis focuses to explore the difference between the real problems and the solutions possible and the macro problems, which require group and organization effort.

Before venturing further with the analysis of the stories, let us first discuss how stories are important in reflecting an individual's unconscious pattern in role-taking behavior.

Stories are derived from shared norms, values and belief systems. In corporate contexts, they help individuals make sense of their workplace and their reasons for working (O'reilly, 1989). Deal and Kennedy (1982) refer to this shared perspective as the way we do things around here. The analysis of stories has gained increasing credibility among researchers of organizational culture (Wilkins, 1978, Wilkins and Martin, 1979, Martin, 1987, Martin et al, 1983, Schein, 1985).

Stories are seldom factual. Instead, stories reflect what people believe needs to be true. For example, contradiction and exaggeration in individual accounts of a superior's stroke in provoking organizational discord and chaos were uncovered by Feldman (1990). The coloring of actual events reflected a deeper belief that emphasized the superior's role and responsibility for organizational problems and corresponding control of the people. The underlying themes of stories are quite interesting when one considers what the unconscious chooses to remember and tell [Schrank, 1990]. Thus, story elements such as heroes can act as cultural models revealing much of what employees believe needs to be organizationally true. If cultural epics and mythological heroes are the role models, the employees seek such behavior from their own leaders of the organization or their bosses. There leaders and bosses may have a completely different role model as their hero and thus create an immense gap in the expectation and reality.

The above example emphasizes the importance of understanding an individual's cultural norms as they convey them rather than imposing an external standard to understand or analyze them. However, stories allow researchers to examine perceptions that are often filtered, denied or not in an individual's consciousness (Martin, 1982).

Keeping these perspectives, frameworks and continuity of the socio-cultural context constantly influencing the family and as such the role behavior of individuals, the stories are analyzed, interpreted and new behavior anchor in identity is facilitated. This tends to help shed some old patterns of behavior which the individual himself/herself has outgrown, and have become obsolete in terms of functionality and discover relevant behavior patterns anchored in the identity and relevant in the present. The focus is also on the new definitions and meanings of people and systems so that the energy feed from the old ways of working and new behavior can be initiated.

SYNOPSIS OF CHAPTER 3 - STORIES BY MANAGERS

In chapter 3, seven TAT cards are divided into three groups: (a) Group 1 consists of cards 1, 4, 5 and 7 which are stories based on one person or single, individual stories on the cards, (b) Group 2 consists of cards 2 and 6 which show two people on the card in the context of two different background contexts reflecting interface stories, and (c) Group 3 consists of Card 3 which includes many individuals around the same age, age reflecting group stories. Each group has certain common themes and the stories on the seven cards are based on events with social and work environments and people or systems. Analysis and interpretations are done through the identification of dominant themes where events and people are located in a context of social and work settings in which the individual plays their social or work roles.

This chapter is based on a series of workshops and stories gathered from approximately 500 managers who attended 17 workshops across 15 organizations. The emerging themes and issues from all seven cards have been consolidated to give overall assessment and understanding of the managers playing their managerial roles in the context of organizations. The managers were categorized in two levels, namely: (1) Classification based on position of the managers in the organization—(a) junior-level managers, (b) middle-level managers, and (c) senior-level managers; and (2) classification based on the generation-time-based classification (a) managers belonging to the decade of the '90s and (b) managers belonging to the millennium decade—2000 onwards.

The stories have been analyzed according to the card groups, viz. level of the manager. These have been analyzed into 1-person, 2-persons and group stories and overall themes have been consolidated. As such, an overall analysis is done for junior, middle and senior-level managers.

CHAPTER 3

STORIES BY MANAGERS

Introduction

The determination of the relationship between the story and the storyteller is the keystone of analyses and interpretations of the stories. This relationship between fantasy, reality and personality is highly complex. TAT situations call for imagination and then translating the imagination into the ongoing reality of the situation. The individual is asked for something more than his fleeting responses. He is invited to share his private fantasies about life, people, relationships and meanings which he/she has given. He is called upon to interpret his behavior, feelings and expectations of individuals represented pictorially. It is for this reason that the individual in his interpretation of the lives of these characters may expose fragments of his own history, his contemporary behavior and his future expectations and aspirations. The stories may reveal his public behavior, those facets shared only with intimates and private feelings guarded against any public scrutiny as well as wishes whose existence has been somehow guarded against even the individual's own awareness.

In a working environment of an organization where there is immense competition and silent evaluations and judgments of each other based on social, cultural, family or educational backgrounds and exposure to the external environment, all these converge in the individual's role and interfaces across roles and relationships in the shared workspace. In order to explore and understand the work-related dynamics in the organization space and the relationship across roles, the stories are explored in group settings. This requires immense sensitivity and understanding of the workspace and the participants to articulate which is safe and comfortable to the participant. At the same time, to bring out the issues which need to be discussed, the interpretation and analysis mode only raises questions for them to reflect and engage with as well as come up with some new initiatives, choices and directions for themselves in the workspaces.

The stories are analyzed keeping in mind the distinctiveness of the group as well as the level of managers in the organization.

1. Story of one-person situations which are reflected in cards number: 1, 4, 5 and 7

2. Story of two-persons situations which are reflected in cards number: 2 and 6

3. Story of group situations which are reflected in card number: 3

These groups were identified as part of the OD initiative where after the OD study recommendations were made for learning and developmental inputs for different levels of managers in the organization. The recommendations have many components and multiple modules. The first module was based on the TAT. Workshops were held in sequence beginning with the senior-level followed by middle-level and at the junior-level. The workshops used the TAT module as the first central and core methodology. The participants were at the level of middle and senior managers of various organizations. Moreover, the managers were from the same organization. The managers were from the age group of 25 to 55 years of age. These managers were from all walks of life and worked in diverse functions and roles. Across the multiple organizations, a large number of managers had a long association with the organization. The managers older in age had started their career in the organization and there were a few who had joined as laterals. This already had created a context of workspace in the organization. At each level, education created an additional dimension. A large number of managers had joined right after their college education while a few others had obtained postgraduate degrees. A large number of managers had general education while a few others had profession-focused education. This sample represents 15 organizations for which comprehensive diagnostic studies were made. The studies had recommendations for development inputs through workshops. This chapter is based on the inputs gathered from approximately 500 managers who attended 17 workshops across 15 organizations.

Analysis of Tat Cards

The seven cards are grouped into three—

I. **Group 1**

Cards no. 1, 4, 5, and 7 (One-person situation)

II. **Group 2**

Cards no. 2 and 6 (Two-people situation)

III. **Group 3**

Card no. 3 (Group situation)

Each group has certain common themes. Analysis and interpretation of the stories are done through the identification of the dominant themes.

Stories by Managers {According to Card Groups}
Group I—Cards No. 1, 4, 5 & 7
Card No. 1

1. The scene is that of an office in which the executive is amidst the office papers. The photo frame in the picture has the family photograph and is placed prominently on the table. As the table is full of papers, the person is finishing off the office work.

    Description: The story only states what is depicted on the card.

2. A man is looking into a group photo. It may be his family or any other people. He is doing work also. In between, he is looking at the photos. But it is not clear as to what he is doing. He recalls the past.

    Description: The story along with the depiction of the card talks about the state of mind of the person in the picture.

3. A person is sitting in front of a photo frame in the office. He may be an officer/manager. He is watching and thinking about the frame and future. He is thinking about himself and the organization, future growth of the company and planning his work.

    Description: The story talks about the person in the card adding information about his work life, his deep thinking and his future growth and planning.

4. A gentleman working in his own office. The day has begun for work. He loves his family very much. The family photograph is on the desk. He begins his day with his family in mind. He knows that if he works hard and perfectly, his future will be bright. He can give all happiness to his family. He also knows what the family expects and how to fulfill it.

    Description: The story describes the man in the card as a family man fully engrossed in his work to fulfill his family's expectations and happiness.

5. The settings look like an official premise, a glassed chamber in an office. A man dressed in formal clothes is seen sitting on a chair at a desk, his hands on the keyboard, his eyes giving satisfied look at the laptop monitor in front of him, his lips giving a gentle smile. The man could be doing some kind of planning work and seems to be getting much satisfaction from what he is doing.

    Description: The story gives minute details about the card. The story also describes the man's state of mind with expressions and emotions.

Card No.4

1. The man is an athlete with a strong body. The scene has a man climbing on a rope. The effort by the man in climbing the rope has his body completely involved. Would he reach the top?

    Description: The story describes the card. This story states about the physique of the man on the card. This also questions about his capacity to achieve his goals.

2. A person is climbing a very straight mountain with the help of a rope. He seems to be quite young and doing his task with confidence for reaching his goal and finally achieves the goal.

    Description: The story describes the card with further details about the man and his achievement.

3. A man is climbing up a rope and is looking outwards rather than looking up. Therefore, he has either climbed the rope to take a look around from an elevated point or maybe he is just looking around to see things out of curiosity.

    Description: The story states the distracted and curious state of mind of the man on the card.

4. This is a picture of a person climbing a role looking upwards. The person has a strong physique and looks determined to climb the rope and reach the top. The picture gives an impression that the person is grafting through the current problems but determined of the top goal that he has to reach.

    Description: The story describes the man in the card to be very strong physically, he is very ambitious, determined and believes in himself.

5. This is the story of a rope climber and acrobat. He actually comes from the deep jungles. He knows how to swing with the rope and climb trees as this was a part of his way of living. As of now, he has arrived in a city as someone once had told him it is a nice place and he is trying to make a living out of what he knows best. He is trying to amuse people with rope acrobatics. But he is wondering whether to

continue with the struggle of a city or go back to his mother nature. He is trapped between the two cultures.

Description: The story states the profession of the man, his background and future actions. This story also describes his confused state of mind where he is not sure of his own abilities.

Card No.5

1. Sitting in a plane. One person looking outside the window and feeling very pleasant. He looks happy and is enjoying himself like on a successful business trip.

    Description: The story depicts the card and states the theme of success and satisfaction.

2. A middle-aged person is sitting on a chair. He is having a handbook in his left hand. Probably this gentleman is thinking and going through this book. Looking at the confidence on his face, it is obvious that he will finish his task.

    Description: The story clearly describes the card. It also portrays satisfaction and hope for future actions.

3. A middle-aged person is traveling in an airplane sitting near the window of the aircraft and he seems to be happy and relaxed as he is returning after a successful meeting to his office. It seems that he has achieved what he wanted for his organization. He is looking out of the glass window and watching the clouds. He seems to be very happy today.

    Description: The story depicts the card with some more details portraying themes of achievement, accomplishment and reflection on the past, present and future.

4. The transparency shows the top-ranking executive, perhaps MD or CMD traveling in the executive class of the airline. Having gone through the papers in the file he is holding, he is reflecting on the issues raised. Yes, he is satisfied, yet concerned.

Description: The story describes the profession of the man, his lavish living style bringing out themes of reflection and reviewing this present and future.

5. A busy and tired executive is traveling from one town to another by sea or air. He had intended to read a book during travel, but at the moment he is reflecting and thinking about something else. The book lies, almost forgotten, on his lap. Toward the end of the journey, the executive will come out of the reverie/thought process and get on with the job.

    Description: The story describes the card with too many details and possibilities. This story brings out themes of reviewing and reflection mostly.

Card No.7

1. An office scene with one person. Also shown are two tables. The person seems disorganized with his hat and coat kept in the dispatch tray. There are papers all over on his desk.

    Description: The story only states what is depicted on the card.

2. The scene is of some office's staff-area seating arrangement where rows of tables are placed. The gentleman has involved himself in writing some papers. But his hat and suit are kept on his working table rather than keeping on hat stand or hooks. Or he must be given some important work in the early hours of the working day and he didn't find time to do other things. He has directly entered and involved himself in urgent work

    Description: The story describes the card with some more details. It brings out the themes of overengagement in work.

3. In the evening, on one lighted desk out of rows of desks in a room, a man is sitting and completing his work. He is a good worker and knows his job, which is why he has a pleased expression on his face. He has come into the office just to attend to his one job; therefore his

hat and coat are lying on his desk. He will complete this job shortly; switch off the lights and leave.

Description: The story gives out some more details about the card like the man's dedication toward this work; it also reflects success and completion of the task.

4. One senior man is working in his office. He has kept his hat on the table. He is busy with his work. It may be after office hours. Because clerks are going home in time and officers have to work for completing tasks kept pending by clerks or for checking purposes. There are no other staff members in the office. An ash-tray can be seen in the picture and also cigarette is there. But there are no papers in the paper basket.

Description: The story portrays the ambiance of the card like about the office working hours. This story brings out the theme of overwork.

5. This is a picture of the office of an executive. He seems to be busy with his work. Nobody is around. At one end, a typewriter is there. The cabin housekeeping is very poor and not in order. The chair is far ahead of him. The table on which he works looks very bad and unorganized. The person is neglecting other things around him and likes to work in his own way. He is a self-centered personality and he wants to complete the task of preparing the final report on production problems immediately. He does it and gets satisfaction.

Description: The story gives out too many details about the card. It reflects the themes of overwork, extreme focus and satisfaction.

Emerging Themes From Stories (Cards 1, 4, 5 and 7)

The stories from the one-person situations of cards 1, 4, 5 and 7 provide the participants the situations to explore and reflect on their role map, their mindset and definition of the job and role that they are using at work situations. This also reflects how they are engaging with performance. Analysis of the stories written is done based on the absence/presence of certain aspects, which are the pulls of the situation presented to them. Moreover, the situations bring out the participants' maps and definitions they hold of their role and interface with the organization.

1. Ambition, sincerity and hard work.

2. Need for recognition, affirmation and approval. There is also a need for guidance, direction, support. {This is part of the interface but managers often bring this need in the one-person setting.}

3. Locus of control—internal/external and acceptance of job role and job satisfaction.

4. Sense of adventure and discovery.

5. Personal philosophy and ability to channelize energy.

6. Relationship between primary and secondary system and expectation of personalized relationships in the work-front {again this is part of interface but often the systematic expectations become linked with their own individual job, role and performance setting}.

7. Vision for future growth.

8. Target/goal orientation and clarity of job/role/performance.

9. Fear/acceptance of success or/and failure.

10. Expectations from self, rigidity/flexibility and ability to be assertive and take initiatives.

11. Guarding of work/lack of designation.

    Essentially, the one-person situation stories reflect the participants' role map, personal or role definitions perspective on the organization structure, directions of growth and the new roles as well as processes.

Stories by Managers—Group 2—Card No. 2 & 6

Card No. 2

1. It is a picture of an office room. Two persons are discussing some matter. Both of them seem to be confident. There is a huge photo of someone behind these two persons. Faces of the persons indicate that some serious discussion is going on.

    Description: The story only states what is depicted on the card.

2. There are two persons in a room. An older man is discussing something with a gentleman who seems to be quite young. In this room, one photograph (framed) is there on the wall. Probably he may be the head of these two persons. I feel they are discussing very seriously to resolve very technical problems with logic/facts and figures.

    Description: The story states what is depicted in the card with the relationship theme across the hierarchy.

3. Picture of an office of a family-oriented business group. The younger man (son) is explaining in detail the progressive results achieved for all areas to the father and the performance of the company. The father has suggested some of the important key result areas—the son listens carefully and thinks about planning actions to achieve excellent results. A picture of the founder is seen on the wall.

    Description: The story gives out the description of the card with some more details. It gives out themes of the relationship between father and son, of expectations and of control.

4. An aged gentleman is talking something to another gentleman who is standing in front of a window as if he was looking outside of the window but as and when the old gentleman started talking to him he looks into the background. There is a big portrait in the backside of the older gentleman. He speaks about tradition. That older gentleman is narrating his thoughts to his junior. The discussion can be translated down the line properly.

Description: The story describes the card as a formal setting bringing out themes around relationships between superior and subordinate, of tradition and hierarchy.

5. An elderly consultant/lawyer is explaining a necessary but difficult decision to a young businessman, possibly who has inherited the business from the founder (whose painting is on the wall). The young businessman is hearing but not listening, as he does not like what he is hearing. Possibly the lawyer is telling him some ground realities, which are true (as indicated by his open palms). Eventually, the young businessman will come around (at least partly) to the view of his lawyer.

    Description: The story gives out too many possibilities portrayed in the card. The formal setting, superior-subordinate relationship, and of control.

Card No.6

1. Two persons are there in the picture. One old person is seated on the fence. One young executive is talking with him, standing in front of the old person.

    Description: The story only states what is depicted on the card.

2. The scene is of some countryside, not of the city and the two gentlemen are father and son or friends. The one in the suit seems to be discussing personal matters which the other one is listening to seriously.

    Description: The story describes the setting of the card, brings out the possible relationship between the two men.

3. A son seems to be enjoying his break in the countryside (farmhouse) and his father seems to remain in his same work. The expected outcome would be positive thought by the son with a relaxed frame of mind.

Description: The story describes the relationship between father and son and the positive interaction and attitude between the two men.

4. Two persons are meeting near a Farm House. They are in a very relaxed mood. They are talking in a light manner. They are not discussing any serious problem. It looks like they met to enjoy some good time after solving a serious problem successfully.

    Description: The story doesn't describe any relationship between the two persons. The story only brings out interactions and attitudes between them.

5. The situation is of one old person and one young person sitting. The old person is standing near the young person. The young person is sitting on the fence and he is listening to some advice very calmly. The young man is very serious about it.

    Description: The story describes the relationship across generations; this brings out the themes of attitude, interaction and authority.

Themes on Card 2 & 6—Two-Persons Situation

The stories from the two-person situations on cards 2 and 6 provide the participants with situations to explore and reflect on their nature and meaning of relationships. The stories they wrote also reflected their attitudes, expectations and residues around relationships especially hierarchical relationships, authority relationships and meanings given to organizational structures, systems and processes. Moreover, the situations brought out the participants' emotional tonality as the relationships unfolded. Analysis of the written stories is done based on the emergent themes and absence or presence of interfaces in social and work settings.

1. Nature of superior-subordinate relationship {roles played by each in the relationship like traditional and authoritarian, modern and participative, etc.}.

2. Nature of social relationships like a father-son relationship.

3. The interface {positive or negative} between the superior and subordinate.

4. The interface (positive or negative) between father/superior and son/subordinate.

5. The construction of hierarchy present and used by the employees in the organizations.

6. Type of communication: upward/downward.

7. Space for dialog and discussion.

8. Work system—open/closed.

9. Level of understanding between the senior and subordinate.

10. Relationship: a single person or mutually shared by both.

11. Presence of tension and conflict and its resolution or non-resolution.

12. Delegating, sharing or owning of responsibilities.

13. Ability for both to be problem and solution-focused.

14. Sheltering, protection, nurturing, caring as part of the role of superior.

15. Tolerance in relationship and openness to be in a performance space.

16. Hope for future relationships redefined.

17. Coherence and congruence in fulfilling tasks and performance.

Essentially, the two-persons stories reflect the issues around relationships between the self and others and self and the system. They revolve around legitimacy and illegitimacy of hierarchy and authority exercised by the senior and experienced by the senior. Although the managers expect guidance and direction, they tend to be ambivalent about the authority from the seniors.

Stories by Managers—Group 3—Card No.3

1. There are six persons in the room. Some are standing and looking outside the window. Some persons are sitting on the chairs and discussing an issue which can be solved by the consensus of all. One gentleman who is standing on the right-hand side of the table is having something in his hand. They are sharing one another's views.

    Description: The story states what is depicted on the card describing the different posture and actions of the people.

2. Six executives are there around the table. Five are sitting. One is standing behind. They are discussing target production and target planning for next year.

    Description: The story states that the card has a formal setting which revolves around achievement and results.

3. The group of the seven executives is discussing an important matter. One executive of the group is viewing outside from the window. Maybe is thinking about the topic or he is not interested in the topic. One member is expressing his views on the topic while others are discussing and planning to put the same into action.

    Description: The story depicts the formal scene where executives are into formal interaction and interaction is about planning and execution.

4. There were seven persons: five senior managers and two plant in-charges. They were discussing to increase production and recoveries by decreasing the production cost. One plant-in-charge is standing near the window after completion of the plant discussion. The other plant-in-charge is discussing with the senior managers regarding plant constraints and downtime, bottlenecks of the plant. If this constraint is overcome, downtime goes down and production and recoveries will increases. Finally, they decided to take stepwise action to overcome these constraints.

Description: The story depicts the group setting where colleagues are discussing official matters. The theme revolves around teamwork and accomplishment.

5. A meeting is going on in the office. There were six persons. One was looking outside through windows. Another person was standing near the table and the other four persons were sitting. Faces of the persons indicate that the discussion is on some serious matter and the person looking outside seems to be not agreeing with others' points of view.

Description: The story depicts the formal setting in the office. It states the interpersonal relationship among colleagues bringing out differences in the teamwork.

Themes on Card 3 Group Situations

The stories from the group situation are from Card 3. The card provides the participants a situation to explore and reflect on the nature and meaning of peer relationships. The stories they write reflect their ability to work together as colleagues and how they accept each other's strengths and limitations and/or are supportive or withholding from each other. The stories also bring out the residues of relationships about siblings and peers and align themselves with the tasks and performance required from them for the organization. Often the stories reflect social settings and/or work settings.

In general, Card 3 analyses views on tasks, policies, strategies and growth of the organization. Additionally, it is also used to determine the following:

1. Social Groups
2. Work Groups
3. Group anchored by a leader or a hierarchical role position
4. Leaderless Group

5. Group interaction—hostile/friendly and lack of active participation, withdrawal, disengagement

6. Dynamics of exclusion and inclusion, absence/presence of team-orientation and avoidance of cooperative conflict, and/or passivity and indifference

7. Fragmentation and/or coherence within the group and inter-linkage between groups/functions/discussions

8. Search for leadership or an anchor/decision-maker and establishment of the hierarchy, leadership, etc. as part of the processes of a group

9. Speed and quality of decision-making, peer-linkages for tasks and performance and result-orientation

10. Group participation and interaction and group dynamics between social relations {friends} or collegiate relations at work

11. Creation/lack of pressure and stress

12. Individualism and boundary between private and public lives

Essentially, this group's stories reflect the individuals' social skills in a group setting be it social or work. The stories bring out the comfort or discomfort of contributing empathy, responsibility and tolerance of working in groups. Most importantly, the stories reflect the space taken by the individual in group settings.

Overall, the seven stories put together bring out a pattern of roles, definitions, meanings and maps of people and situations held by the participants. The stories reflect the patterns of resolution or non-resolution, and the ability to bring closure to tasks and jobs on hand through performance and commitment. An analysis is also done based on whether there is a positive or negative resolution or if there is any resolution.

These workshops were held as a result of OD intervention in approximately 15 organizations. Participants of the workshop were the junior-level, middle-level and senior-level of managers. In each module, there were between 20–25 managers across the same level.

The workshops reflect a decade of OD studies followed by workshops {Parikh, I.J}.

The workshops were held off-site.

1. The participants reflected middle-level managers of 1990s

2. The participants reflected middle-level managers of 2000s

3. The participants reflected senior-level managers of 1990s

4. The participants reflected middle-level managers of 2000s

In this chapter, the topics and themes for each set of cards (i.e. Cards no. 1, 4, 5 and 7, Cards no. 2 and 6, Card no. 3) have been illustrated. In this chapter, the TAT stories of the sample have been analyzed using the guidelines stated earlier. The analysis has been broken down into two steps:

I. **Step 1:** The overall themes have been consolidated as under the system of classification. Thereby, an overall analysis is done for Junior, Middle and Senior-level Managers based on the time of testing.

II. **Step 2**: Stories have been analyzed according to the card groups. Thus, junior-level managers have been analyzed into three groups—Group 1 consists of cards 1, 4, 5 and 7; Group 2 consists of cards 2 and 6; Group 3 consists of Card 3.

Junior-Level Managers

Cards No. 1, 4, 5 & 7

The workshops first discussed the stories at the content-level analysis. The discussions then led to the analysis of stories as to what their meanings meant to the participant. These were some of the meanings and themes as they emerged from the faculty analysis and discussions.

1. Ownership of self, task and system are missing. The protagonists in the stories seldom play dynamic roles in the process of initiating change and/or development of ideas, concepts, etc. This is indicative

of the managers' focus on the job and lack of clarity (both personal and/or organizational) for future growth.

2. Most of the stories are descriptive in nature. The managers have described the settings as depicted or visible in the situation rather than the themes and motives of the characters. This brings out the over-emphasis on the givers especially with regard to taking initiatives and actions. The junior-level managers are unable to initiate action plans for themselves and do not have a broader understanding of the totality of organizations.

3. The descriptive stories also indicate the emphasis on micro-issues. Such a focus inhibits the managers from obtaining a macro organizational perspective.

4. Many stories have no resolutions or outcomes. The stories end in mid-sentences or fade away into the nothingness of unstated incomplete aspirations. They bring out the trend of *trying to, will compete,* etc. However, there is no mention of this being converted into actions or positive resolutions or outcomes.

5. Most managers feel overengaged and under-utilized. Many stories depict the culture of staying late at work which conflicts with the pulls of the family. Although the managers work hard, there is no evidence of their work being recognized, or their experiencing appreciation or their outcomes being successful.

6. The stories highlight the significance of people-orientation as compared to task-orientation. Many stories depict the fatigue and stress generated by tasks. Some stories reflect the isolation and aloneness of working and families being positive emotionally sustaining strength.

7. Problems are perceived to be much larger than solutions. While task-related themes may have problems in instrument or performance, there is no mention of any solutions to these problems.

8. Most of the stories portray the managers' need for guidance, direction and support. The "self" is often perceived as helpless and deserving

sympathy. Managers deal with situations by withdrawing and/or resigning.

There is a general sense of apprehension and confusion about their individual capabilities and capacities. This causes the managers to be caught up with individual issues as opposed to the task and organizational issues.

9. Organizational space belongs to the top management and workers with very little space for the officers. Work means appreciation and acknowledgment from others. The individuals perceive themselves as small and inadequate.

Cards No. 2 & 6

Formal Setting

1. The mode of interaction between the superior and subordinates is primarily in the form of instructions, explanations, advice, orders or demands. Thus, superiors tend to be autocratic and domineering. The interface does not create space for exploration from both parties. As a result, there is little or no space for participative discussions.

2. The stories bring out the nature of the relation between the superiors and subordinates. Most of the stories depict a single person relationship, in which there is no space for dialog and discussion. Due to the distance between the superiors and subordinates, there is difficulty in dealing with issues such as nonperformance, negative attitudes, etc.

3. The superior is often shown as questioning, forcing, firing, instructing, advising and warning and seldom seen as someone who explains his actions. The subordinate, on the other hand, is shown as ignoring, arguing, insulting, disrespecting or passively listening. Obedience and compliance with internal anger is the primary mode of interface. Blame and accusation also emerge in the interface.

4. A strong vertical hierarchy exists between the superiors and subordinates. Hierarchy is never extended into a meaningful relationship and is primarily characterized by a one-way communication channel—where there is a downward flow of communication from top to bottom. To add to this, communication is focused only on the achievement of tasks. This causes the subordinates to develop disrespect and disregard for authority.

5. A low level of understanding exists between the superiors and subordinates. This results in ineffective modes of tension and conflict resolution. The impact of performance appraisals is influenced by this. Thus, evaluations are meant only for criticism or giving negative opinions and not for appreciation.

Informal Setting

6. Informal settings are presented with open communication channels with a lack of hierarchy. In such a setting, individuals have large spaces for dialog and discussion and have the freedom to express themselves. There is a healthy interaction, which cultivates an amicable and pleasant environment.

7. Although the stories are non-hierarchical in nature (in the traditional sense), an informal hierarchy does seem to exist. However, this form of hierarchy is horizontal in nature and thus has fewer layers. The communication channels are more flexible and open to participative discussions.

8. The stories bring out themes of advice, guidance and suggestions in both, hierarchical and non-hierarchical relationships. A healthy and warm relationship between the two individuals is depicted in most stories

Card No. 3

1. Card 3 provides the setting to determine the nature of group involvement and interaction. The managers' stories reflect the

presence of healthy group dynamics. The friendly and congenial atmosphere leads to successful outcomes of group interactions.

2. Some stories portray a non-hierarchical structure. In such stories, even task-related themes do not have a formal hierarchy. However, the inter-linkages between the group members are not clear. At times, the interface quality can be cooperative, while at other times, it can be hierarchical and conflict-ridden.

3. Some stories reflect a common purpose/goal among the officers. However, on the whole, there is a search for leadership—most of the group interactions end in chaos and confusion. There is a need to increase the speed of decision-making.

4. There is an absence of interactive communication between the group members. Accountability toward group members is nonexistent. The group interactions are classified by defensive behavior. The need to prove one right comes out strongly in several stories.

   There is no collective responsibility to maintain group discipline. This results in withdrawal or disengagement. There are few members who take initiatives.

5. Task completion neglects the softer aspects of group dynamics. In the process of completing tasks, the interface, inter-linkages and interpersonal relationships get influenced in an adverse manner. The focus is on the final product rather than the processes involved.

Officers Group

The officers are a large group of individuals who feel quite oppressed, demoralized and demotivated. They are a level above the workers but feel their privileges are few and expectations from them are more. The workers are at a better advantage and demands[2] from them are less. Half

---

2   {Parikh, I.J, (1997), Organization Cultural Transformation Process, A study of Mahindra & Mahindra Tractor Division, January – May 1997, Indian Institute of Management, Ahmedabad}

of the officers' cadre is promoted from within while the other half is directly recruited. The group is skilled but carries fears and apprehensions about the security of their jobs. They feel that the workers do not respect them and the management does not value them. They do not receive the pampering like the workers from the management and support from the union. All they receive are the demands for targets and production and restraints and constraints.

A group of 140 were asked to leave. This generated fear and anxiety and an attitude of compliance and surrender to the instructions from the seniors. The officers' interface with the workers is that of cajoling and pleading. Any change requires intervention and mediation by the union. The officers do not have any direct interface with the workers which makes it difficult for them to exercise authority. They can only make requests and no support is available from the management to curb indiscipline among the workers.

The workers have felt that the officers take away the credit of their suggestions, innovativeness and creativity. The workers believe that the new officers do not know the machines. The machine is the property of the workers and the officers do not acknowledge or give credit to the workers.

The officers feel they continue to do hands-on work of all the work the workers do not do. They double up as workers. They are unable to exercise discipline, more so, those officers who have been promoted from the workers' rank.

Figure 8: Profile of Officers

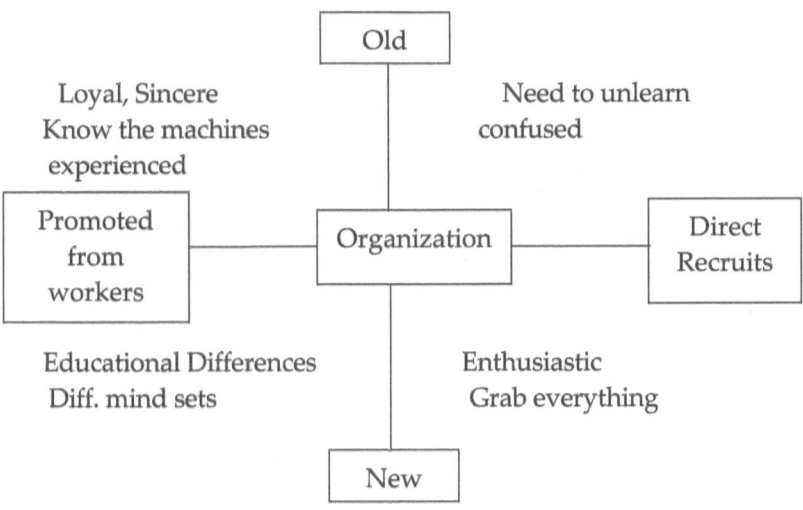

i. Organizations have promotee officers and direct recruits.

ii. The promotee officers are older while direct recruits are younger.

iii. The promotees know the machines and have a traditional mindset of loyalty to the organization and possessiveness of the machine.

iv. The direct recruits are looking for career opportunities and growth.

{Parikh, Indira .J, Organization Cultural Transformation Process, A Study of Mahindra & Mahindra Tractor Division, Indian Institute of Management (Ahmedabad), (Jan – May 1997)}

The role-taking of the promoted and direct recruits is quite distinct and different. Below are given some of the differences in their behavior.

1. Promotee officers feel valued but find themselves as losers as they lose out on OT and union support.

2. Promotee officers find it difficult to exercise authority on the same people who were once their colleagues.

3. The lifestyle of promotee officers has not changed. They continue to live with their earlier colleagues. However, their social status has changed.

4. The new officers are ambitious and career-oriented.

5. The new officers do not know the machines and have to learn the machines from the workers.

6. Officers have to work longer hours as their seniors stay longer hours.

7. Officers do not feel motivated or empowered to do much on their own initiative. Their bosses supervise day-to-day routine operations.

8. Some officers report to two functions. If their seniors get along with their reporting, the interface works well. If they do not, the problems are pushed downward and the officer is under a crossfire of contradictory instructions.

9. Officers are not enthusiastic or excited about their work as they have no control of workers or respect from workers.

10. Officers cannot motivate their workers. They can only talk of output and numbers, plead and cajole. Sometimes the officers end up doing workers' jobs.

11. The officers are demoralized as there has been increasing reluctance on the part of the senior managers to take tough decisions with the workers or decisions anchored in the systemic discipline.

12. Officers are in trouble with the management if they do not produce the numbers and deliver the targets.

13. As the union mediates on every issue officers cannot exercise and/or do not have any authority.

14. The workers have support from the union but the officers do not have support from their seniors.

15. The performance appraisal has no meaning as there is a quota system on promotions. The belief is that only loyalty and

personalized relations with the superiors get the rewards and not merit and hard work.

16. There is a fear of being victimized, so there is a lot of tolerance of indiscipline from workers.

17. There is a lot of mistrust among the officers among themselves as well as upward.

18. The officers feel like a football. They are tossed from the superiors to the workers and by the workers to the top.

19. When the officers are placed in the department there are no systems of induction, communication and procedures. The seniors do not know what to do with them. This creates confusion and the officers feel lost. They lose trust in the management. This experience suggests that the management has done no planning for their induction, orientation and socialization in the organization.

20. There is no discussion or dialog around performance appraisal. The officers are not invited to any discussions with their superiors.

21. The officers formed an association which was largely operative in the plant. This association was largely ignored by the management. Subsequently, 140 officers were asked to leave. This decision of the management has been associated with the decision and action of the officers to form the association. This decision has generated fear and anxiety in the remaining officers and also led to compliance.

22. The officers who interface among themselves, with their seniors and workers require a reorientation. The officers, both promoted within the ranks and direct recruits, need to experience a sense of self-esteem and of being valued for their contributions. Similarly, the whole group needs to acquire an organizational, managerial and supervisory role perspective which is relevant for the times, the organization and the changing environment.

Workers Profile

There are five thousand workers in an organization and they also come from a homogenous regional linguistic background. Most have been with that organization for two to three decades. The workers have witnessed the growth of the organization. They own a sense of pride for being part of ups and downs, stability and turbulence and an overall increase in the numbers of tractors produced.

The workers can be categorized into three different phases. Those who entered in the 1970s, those who joined in 1979 and those who joined in the eighties and after. In the seventies, the organization worked under the policy of price control. The workers employed were under a temporary category and could not/were not confirmed until the organization started doing well. These workers remained uncertain and temporary for a very long time. This uncertainty has left these workers holding the organization as unjust and unfair. More so, when workers who joined in 1979 as trainees were confirmed in two years. The pre-1979 workers see themselves as seniors in the plant. They are older, more experienced and mature and yet some bitterness comes through. They believe they have a better sense of belonging and respect the machines and the organization more than the next generation. The post-1979 are a different group, slightly more educated and with positive attitudes of themselves.

The workers are educated up to class ten or twelve. Some, very few have their wives employed while a large majority is home-based. Most have one to three children. A large number have their children studying in English medium schools. Those who have grown-up children are in polytechnics and some are in engineering colleges. There are a few whose children do not wish to study and may be loitering or unemployed. Some have their children in the same organization and the dynamics of these children as employees creates its own dynamics of visibility, centrality, be allegiance '-dare you-' attitude toward system and authority and overall riding on fathers' own visibility, centrality in the plant. There are rare but existing cases where the father is a worker and the son is an officer. The quality and lifestyle of the organization's workers have improved over the years. Many own their own residential premises. They have the basic amenities of comfortable living. Many own a two-wheeler and some four-wheelers. Their aspirations for their lives and their children's lives have increased. Their ambitions have risen. They are aware of their voice and power to make demands and agreements from the management. They are an intelligent group when discussing the lockout, agitation and demands for OT. They had the following observations to make:

1. The times and decade of the strike and lockout were different. We did not have much to lose and it was do-or-die.

2. We were very surprised that the management gave in to our unreasonable demands.

3. The company wants to make money. Rather than all the earnings go to the shareholders we must get our share.

4. It is our hard work, foil of the sweat and our sacrifice of the family time that there is an increase in the number of goods produced.

5. The workers have become aware of the potentials of their earning capacity and their expertise with the machines. They also know that the young freshly recruited engineers and officers do not know the machines and as such have to learn the knowledge of the machines from them. The workers believe that they hold the ownership of the machines.

6. The workers have many suggestions to offer. However, they feel the officers have the need to exercise authority over them just because they are officers. Some of the workers were upset as they said their ideas were taken over by the officer who got credit for it.

7. The workers are appreciative of all the educational inputs provided by the organization and encouragement in upgrading their knowledge and skills.

8. Quality circles are good as they learn from each other and solve the work-related problems.

However, the workers felt that if the organization wants quality products like the Japanese they need to be provided with facilities like Japan and quality of life like Japan.

Union

The union has had its ups and downs in terms of significance, visibility and power. In the sixties, the union was in its nascent phase. Today it has acquired enormous power and significance. For example, there is one union in the organization where membership of the committee and negotiating committee change at the time of each election of the union. The organization's employees feel that the union has acquired enormous powers to which management surrenders. Between what is termed as management and union the rest of the employees across levels of management have to accommodate, adjust, conform and hope for the best that targets will be met. Like the seniors in the management, the union leaders also have acquired enormous individual and personal power to influence decisions of the organization.

The nineties was a turning point for the union in the history of the same organization where the whole issue of management and union acquired a new meaning. In 1977, the union had reached an agreement on the bonus issues with the management. However, the workers were unhappy and were agitating. They took the usual route of go-slow and held meetings at the gate. Some workers broke the discipline and the management declared a lockout. The lockout lasted for 37–40 days. Eventually, the settlement was done between the top management and the union leaders where workers and the union were the largest beneficiaries. This settlement eroded a lot of authority of the managers as well as the then leaders of the plant. The whole settlement left residues of dissatisfaction, win-lose situation and a sense of betrayal in the managers. The legacy of this settlement and the price of this settlement hangs heavily across the organization even today.

The unintended and unanticipated consequences of the settlement have accumulated over time and have grown into a big giant uncontrolled and unaccountable creating havoc in today's times of competitive environment. Over time the workers have acquired a belief that they are indispensable to the organization. They have also realized that the power of the negotiating committee comes from them. The traditional historical process of workers believe that union is their support; the workers today believe that union is there to do what the workers ask them to do. They can have all the licenses and the union's role is to protect them no matter what they do is right or wrong.

Today's new committee with many new members is attempting to establish itself. At present they have limited control over the workers. According to the workers, the leaders are selected by the workers. The role of the negotiating committee becomes that of getting what the workers want for the. The committee does not and cannot exercise its discretion to judge what is organizationally right.

The Union-Management Interface

The union elections were held recently and there has been a set of new leaders who have been elected. This set of people has come after nine years. This group is still grappling with the roles and stances they need to take with the management. The motto with which they came into power is the theme of *PARIVARTAN* meaning change. However, this group is still to decide the stance they will take with the management. The union-management interface has its roots in the history of the organization's growth and the evolution of work culture in the same organization.

One way of looking at the management-union interface is the perception of management and union about each other.

Table 1

Management perceived by Union	Union perceived by Management
Management is benign/benevolent and not businesslike.	Union is good.
Does not punish indiscipline.	Every change has to be discussed sanctioned by the Union.
Always for increase in production.	Demands a price for any change. Can talk to the union.
Management disregards quality.	Management's perspective understood by union.
Management provides learning opportunities.	Sensitive, s forget what they learn very quickly.
Faith in the management require integrity of speech and action.	Workers are clever and intelligent.
Keep comparing with the situation in Japan.	Do not do work. They sleep on the job.
Company gives more to the shareholders.	OT on duty.
Company makes us pay more tax, does not give tax benefits.	If union does not get its way they threaten to slow down.
Only wants production; does not give time for maintenance.	The workers know that this is a captive plant; so they negotiate their terms.
Introduction of BPR is to reduce manpower.	Union knows BPR is the only way for organization to survive.

{Parikh, Indira .J, Organization Cultural Transformation Process, A Study of Mahindra & Mahindra Tractor Division, Indian Institute of Management (Ahmedabad), (Jan – May 1997)}

Both the management and the union consider each other to be reasonable and rational. However, given the history of their interface, neither wants to confront the other or push each other which will lead to entrenchments or tough, non-negotiable stances. This cautious and tentative approach with each other makes the rest of the managerial and supervisory cadre helpless. The systematic task and performance discipline gets eroded, the authority of the supervisors and managers is vitiated and the price paid by the organization for peace is high.

Figure 9 suggests that the management-union interface gets caught with emotional-rational responses with each other. The union is looking for personal monetary gains while the management is looking for organizational growth and responds to the competitive business environment. The union and the workers do understand and accept the rationality of growth; however, they also want their lifestyles to improve. The only way possible for this is through the increase in remuneration through OT. The management is caught with the historical baggage of the interface. Both get caught with the dynamics of emotional-rational expectations.

Figure 9: Emotive Cognitive Interface: Management & Union

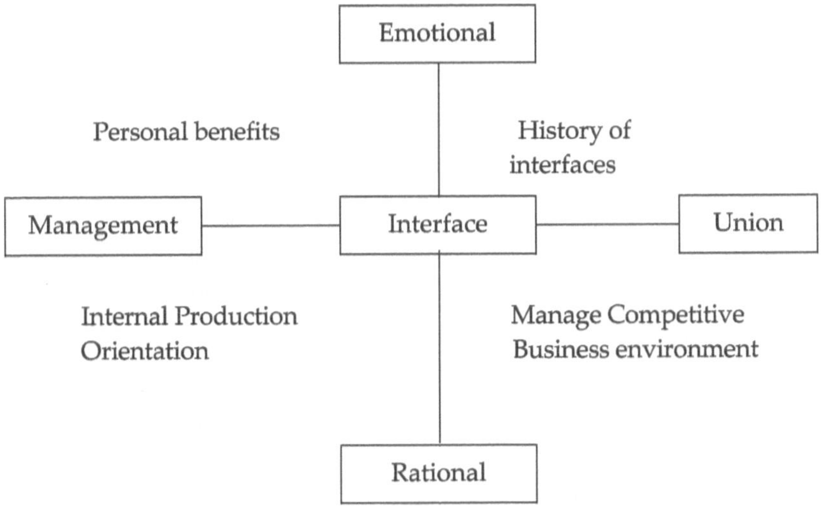

---

i.   The union is caught with seeking personal benefits
ii. The management is caught with the history of dysfunctional interfaces
iii. The union understands the task-orientation but seeks personal gains
iv. The management is responding to a competitive business environment

---

{Parikh, Indira .J, Organization Cultural Transformation Process, A Study of Mahindra & Mahindra Tractor Division, Indian Institute of Management (Ahmedabad), (Jan – May 1997)}

The organization does become vulnerable in this tug of war. The price of peace and status quo adds to the immense dysfunctionality in performance. However, the management needs to recognize that the union and its membership of workers are equally vulnerable in the sense they have acquired a lifestyle for which they would also not want to be the losers. The price of war is equally high for the workers and the union.

Figure 10 elaborates the figure 9.

Figure 10: Union-Management Interface

i.   The union wants a price for change

ii. The management's earlier focus was social welfare

iii. The union is intelligent and acknowledges the need for change
     but also realizes managements need growth

iv. The management is visualizing to become global

{Parikh, Indira .J, Organization Cultural Transformation Process, A Study of Mahindra & Mahindra Tractor Division, Indian Institute of Management (Ahmedabad), (Jan – May 1997)}

The rationale for a realistic work discipline in the organization and collaboration for a dynamic and performing organization can be made possible. At present, there is goodwill from both sides and the managerial cadre is looking for direct interface with the workers for tasks and performance and not constant mediation by the union. Figure 11 depicts the current interface between the managers and the union.

Figure 11: Managers - Union Interface

Managers  Workers

Interface

Mediated by the Union

{Parikh, Indira .J, Organization Cultural Transformation Process, A Study of Mahindra & Mahindra Tractor Division, Indian Institute of Management (Ahmedabad), (Jan – May 1997)}

In any system, one group or the other is going to push the system to test the limits of the system when the system draws the boundary and realistically dialogs and negotiates as well as exercises its own legitimate authority the chances are that systemic discipline and respect for the system and individuals can emerge. The organization and the employees are ready for such a stance; what is necessary is sagacity, wisdom and a determinant to pay the price for the choice of the organization's work culture and work ethos.

Middle-Level Managers—1990's

1. The managers view themselves as ambitious, hardworking, responsible and capable. However, they believe they are not given enough authority and accountability to be fully effective. They play the role of doers and implementers. This not only makes their work monotonous, routine and mechanical but the managers also lose their energy and involvement. The managers learn the art of making their seniors accountable and as such increase the work pressure of their seniors

2. This group of middle-level managers finds it difficult to take initiatives and be assertive. There are many internal and organizational inhibitions and barriers with respect to decision-making and problem-solving. Handwork does not counterbalance the lack or absence of confidence and assertiveness. Though the managers work hard and spend more time at work and at their tasks, they do not perceive themselves as making a difference. They also do not sense or experience success. As a result, managers feel demoralized and dissatisfied.

3. Managers are able to identify problems. However, they focus only on a part of the problem, thereby resulting in partial solutions. This leads to the recurrence of the same problems. The problem space in reality is much larger than the solution space. Recurrence of the problems then becomes chronic and there is rarely a feeling of satisfaction of finding full solutions.

4. The managers seek guidance and directions from the seniors. In the absence of an effective senior or a leader, the middle managers experience abandonment. There are few resolutions of problem-situations. The managers wish for a dynamic, demanding and competent superior who would include them and call for their participation and involvement as a department or a team.

5. There is an excessive tendency of the managers to depend on their seniors for solutions. They also wait for guidance and feedback on

their performance, thereby leading to delays in problem-solving and decision-making.

6. Most managers feel that promotion policies are based on personal biases and preferences and do not reflect merit. Those managers who do get promoted do not see any difference in their new role, level of authority and/or responsibility. They continue to do the same job and at the same level.

7. There is an incongruence between the managers' vision and organizational vision. Managers see themselves in a stage of transition, characterized by feelings of confusion and helplessness.

8. There is a lack of system and structure within the organization. The organization has grown by the pull of the opportunities and not much planning. With the recruitment of personnel at the senior-level, organizations are becoming "top-heavy". There is a felt need to redesign organization structures so that there is clarity of directionality and role boundaries.

9. There is a communication gap across departments and levels of management. Communication tends to flow in a downward manner; managers expect and look for social and personalized relationships; when that does not happen, managers experience isolation and a feeling of not being cared for.

10. The dynamics across the social lateral interface are participative, involved and inclusive. However, the dynamics across the formal lateral interface is held and experienced in acceptance/rejection, inclusion/exclusion, and engagement or disengagement.

11. Managers find it difficult to arrive at discussed decisions with a consensus. There is a tendency to push the decision to a higher level.

12. The influence of the primary system—the family, is especially evident in the relation between the managers and their seniors. In the depiction of the social roles, the father is often portrayed as the dominant and authoritative leader while the son is portrayed as the

passive and unresponsive listener. Similarly, managers feel that their seniors are autocratic and exercise sometimes unreasonable authority over them. Thus most managers experience their workspace as belonging only to the seniors—this gets translated into the process of inclusion-exclusion and often withdrawal.

13. There is a fear of confrontation and disagreement as a result of which issues are seldom resolved.

Content Analysis from Stories

1. Managers' clarity on job, task and role is limited. They do not connect the linkages vertically or horizontally.

2. Managers carry the baggage of the history of the organization and their experiences with residues.

3. Many managers had reached a professional plateau—they experience a sense of psychological saturation and stagnation. Most of the middle-level managers, *although physically present*, were psychologically absent as the job they did was routine.

4. The stories reflected the continuity of social structure and traditions where the younger managers, though professionally educated *must* learn from the senior managers, irrespective of their competence, ability or the guiding capacity of the senior managers.

5. The concept of "colleague" had no significance—collegiate relationships were converted very quickly into hierarchical relationships and/or social and friendly gossip sessions.

Analysis of the Stories
Card No. 1, 4, 5 & 7
Middle-level Managers from 1990-1999

The stories largely depict the physical description of the settings:

1. Absence of creativity and innovative ideas.

2. Managers have the potential but they need to be appreciated and validated.

3. There is a fear of being evaluated and judged by the seniors and hence there is a hesitation in trying out new ways of doing things.

4. Most of the stories are work-related where a lot of thinking is done. However, there is very little time spent on planning and strategizing.

5. Very few stories reflect ambitions and aspirations for high achievement and success.

6. The family plays a significant role in the lives of the managers. The family serves as a source of inspiration, support and mobilization to work.

7. Most managers show the potential for growth and success. Most of the stories have a positive resolution/outcome.

8. The managers explored the nature of the problem and discovered that if they shifted the location of the problem to a larger functional and organizational context they find many alternatives and action choices. Relocation of the problem in a larger context provides the freedom to discover many ways to enlarge the solution space and bind its recurrence.

Figure 12: Problem-Solution Set

Problem Set ⟶ Solution Set

i. The problem set takes up more time and space
ii. The solution set needs to be bigger than the problem set

{Adapted from Parikh, I.J. consultancy (April. 1996)}

The solution set is sought from the problem set which makes the solution smaller and not enduring. The group explored the context in which the problem could be located and as such, find new solutions

Figure 13: Problem – Solution – Relocation

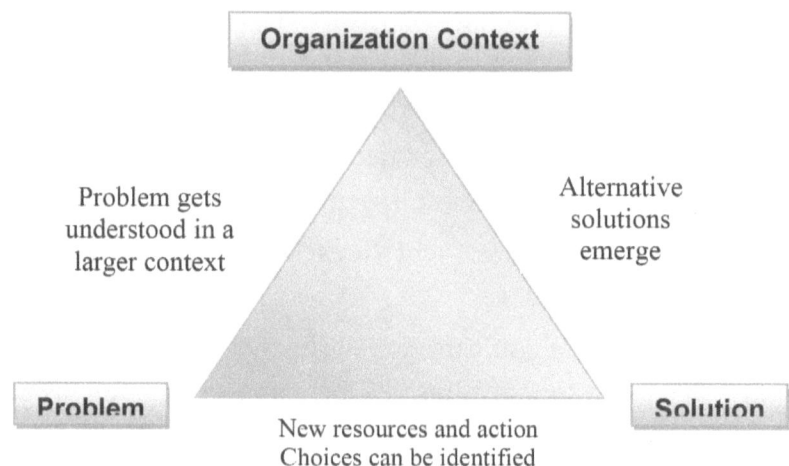

---

i.   Locating the problems in the larger organizational context gives multiple alternatives

ii. The problems are put in an organizational perspective and multiple action choices can emerge

---

{Adapted from Parikh, I.J. consultancy (April. 1996)}

9. **Guarding of work area and lack of delegation:** The tasks and the work area are zealously guarded by some of the managers as suggested by the stories, Absence of delegation is the most obvious manifestation of this phenomenon. In delegating, a threat is perceived to one's own zone of activity within the system and the outcome is not only performing a level or two below the designated grade but is supplemented by no envisioning for either the task or the function.

10. Some stories bring out the trend of 'trying to … will complete', 'sure of success', etc. and at present are in a mode of selecting alternatives, and making new choices. However, there is no evidence that the choice has been converted into action.

11. Many managers are in a mode of remembering their past and are finding the present situation not up to the mark or as per their

expectations, and therefore, prefer remaining engaged in routine work only.

12. Stories bring about the dedication, sincerity and hardworking nature of the individuals. But mostly stories speak more of intentions than results.

Cards No. 2 & 6

Middle-Level Managers—from 1990–1999

1. The managers find it difficult to accept the authority of the superiors as legitimate who know more about the jobs {more so among the younger managers}.

2. Middle managers see themselves as carrying the bulk of the organization on their shoulders whereas the seniors tend to advise and reprimand.

3. There is excessive dependence of the middle managers on their seniors to give them feedback on their performance, thus leading to delays in problem-solving and decision-making.

4. They continue to carry the social patterns of authority and bring those to the workplace {work organization}.

5. The stories reflect the continuity of social traditions whereby the young man must learn from the senior whether the seniors have the capacity to guide or not. In the absence of adequate guidance, there is confusion with regard to goals, objectives and targets.

6. Social relationships (father-son) are carried into the work-setting {superior-subordinate}. The younger person comes through most often as helpless, giving in and passive. The stories around the social relationship of father-son revolve around heritage and organization practices initiated by the father or the earlier generation. The son takes the role of a passive listener holding back the feelings at the self and experiential level.

7. The workspace is seen and experienced as the space belonging to the seniors. It is the superior who owns the space and the subordinate

who enters the space which belongs to the superior. This quickly gets translated into processes of exclusion-inclusion and takes away the initiative and enthusiasm of the subordinates.

8. The stories portray the inhibitions in openly interacting with their superiors around tasks. There seems to be unidirectional communication top-down. While the seniors end up advising, the subordinate is frozen into silence and carrying resentment, anger and hostility.

9. The managers find the interface with superiors as non-negotiable. The human sensitivities and touch are missing from work-related interfaces and dominantly the focus is on tasks. Generating human relatedness becomes difficult in this organization.

10. Authority interface is filled with tension. There are many unresolved issues with authority; there is a transfer of unresolved issues from social settings to workspace especially with the younger generation.

   Authority interface laced with tension: Among young managers who are on the fast track, the authority interface carries with it its own share of tensions. Unresolved issues with authority in social systems are carried over into the work systems. The young managers are prone to complain of a "Boss who just does not understand". The mindset takes over that the boss's viewpoint must necessarily clash with the subordinate. The boundaries in such a relationship are constantly being negotiated with no satisfactory resolution in sight. The manager feels his boss curbs because he resents the resources of the subordinates while the boss feels the manager is too self-righteous and a know-it-all.

11. The perspectives held by the superior and subordinate are quite different as the experience and expectation bases differ. It is difficult to find a shared understanding between the two.

   The majority of issues are around hierarchy and exercising authority in the traditional form. The underlying expectation of the younger individual which is not stated but held is that the older/ father/

superior will be open to listening, give space for experiencing and experimenting to have a dialog, and listen and respect the younger person. The interface space between younger and older is filled with past unresolved issues and residues of hurt and anger. The older/ senior is unable to go listening and initiating a dialog.

Card No. 3

Middle-Level Managers—from 1990–1999

1. The stories by the managers reflected stereotyped social meanings to each other's behavior. There were no collegiate task-relationship processes reflected in the stories. Underlying there was a strong pull to look for an anchor and a leader who could make the decisions and provide directions to which they could disagree and feel oppressed. Below are presented the key themes which reflect the underlying attitudes of the managers to groups and teams.

2. The stories with a resolution are of informal gatherings.

3. Meetings are for tasks but largely focused on discussions and at best planning. The decision gets taken only when a senior is postulated and the senior takes the decision.

4. The stories reflected the following processes.

   If you disagree—leave.

   Do not discuss differences—remain quiet, compromise or grumble.

5. By and large, stories are descriptive and frozen meanings are given to actions. For example, standing near a door means leaving, uninterested and indifferent. Looking out of the window means indifference, disagreement and uninvolved.

6. Though there are seven men shown in the picture most managers saw only five or six. The group explored whether they had left themselves out or those managerial qualities necessary for an organization could be represented by that person who was not a part of the group. The group then explored how they could evolve and work as a team.

7. The issues which emerged were:

    i. How does the group manage differences?

    ii. How do the inter-functional links get established and operationalized?

    iii. How do managers collaborate as a group?

    iv. How do they arrive at consensus decisions and implement the decisions taken?

8. The stories reflect the absence of team-orientation. Stories suggest that most managers like to be lone performers or at best foster dyad relationships with the boss or one of the peer group members. Group work, thinking together or seeking each other as a resource is largely absent. Colleagues as a concept is very limited and of no significance. However, it requires significance emotionally in terms of comparison, discrimination, competition and denials.

9. The search is for leadership in the group. Without the leadership, the group does not get mobilized nor takes any decisions.

10. Participation and involvement by every member of the group are difficult. There is some member who carries the baggage of the history and the past and feels excluded, rejected, disengaged and withdrawn.

11. Collegiate relationships get converted into hierarchical authority relationships.

    The following figure illustrates the collegiate interface

Figure 14: Collegiate Interface

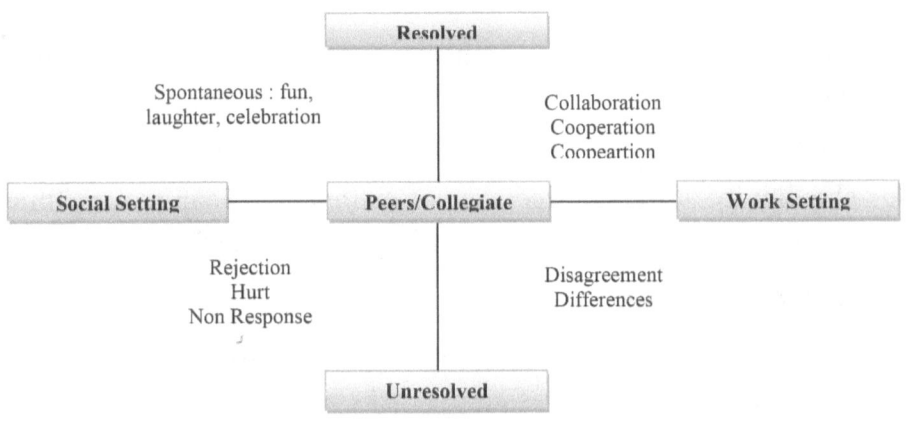

i. The interface in a social or work-setting is either resolved or unresolved.

ii. In the social setting, resolution creates spontaneous fun, laughter and celebration.

iii. In the social setting, rejection, hurt and nonresponse leads to non-resolution.

iv. In the work-setting, resolution creates cooperation, collaboration and consensus.

v. Disagreements, differences and conflicts lead to non-resolution

{Adapted from Parikh, I. J (Phase II, May. 1996)

Middle-Level Managers – 2000 onwards

Issues Identified by the Middle-Level Managers 1990s

Organizational Issues

1. Managers have clarity of job, role and performance. However, a boundary of what is their role exists and this creates confusion and

often there are overlaps. The managers experience erosion of each other's roles.

2. The salary structure is unrealistic as compared to the market conditions.

3. The physical working environment is unsatisfactory.

4. The dignity of the managers is not maintained. Seniors sometimes shout at them in the presence of others and also their subordinates.

Managerial Issues

1. Managers have clarity about their job but are uncertain about the interface and linkages across tasks and functions and overall organizational perspectives and directions.

2. Managers are overengaged in routine jobs and lack action-orientation.

3. There is more focus on problems and less on solutions. This leads to partial resolutions and recurrence of the same problems over and over again.

4. Managers are preoccupied with seeking and receiving acceptance. They are caught with the social code where acceptance is by the virtue of being a family member.

Interface Issues

1. Managers have many expectations from their seniors and they lack the ability to maturely handle the situation involving seniors or subordinates.

2. Managers become touchy and sensitive and often carry hurt feelings while managers need not be fearful of differences, assertiveness and conflicts but must be able to deal with differences.

3. Managers expect action choices, decisions and directionality from top management.

4. Teamwork or group meetings automatically got converted to hierarchical situations when a senior member or group coordinator took charge as part of the team.

Middle-Level Managers—2000's

1. Managers were searching for an anchor in a leader—a leader who could take decisions and provide guidance and directions to them so that they could get on with their jobs. Managers experienced a lack of clarity with respect to tasks and roles. They knew their jobs but waited for instructions.

2. Managers felt that they were not in charge of their own tasks: They were largely dependent on their seniors who would give them instructions as to what to do and how to do. Accountability rested only with their seniors but the responsibility with them. The stories reflected that very often the seniors did not take initiatives. There are frequent delays in decision-making and as such delay in meeting targets and deadlines.

3. Managers experienced constraints and did not feel valued by their seniors.

4. Decision-making often was centralized, as most organizations were highly structured and dependent on the top role holder.

5. The primary system—family—played an important role in the relations and interface between juniors and seniors. The seniors exerted authority over their subordinates who remained passive and unresponsive to the interface

Content Analysis From Stories

1. Managers have a logical and rational approach toward their work and believe they can deliver.

2. They have a positive attitude toward their tasks but feel marginalized when it comes to recognition.

3. There is a minimum emphasis on teamwork and inter-functional linkages and as such very few issues get resolved.

4. Meetings are seldom productive—they are largely focused on discussions that go on and on. Decisions taken are seldom implemented.

Analysis of the Stories
Cards No. 1, 4, 5 & 7
Middle-level Managers 2000 onwards

1. Most of the stories on situation-1 depicted family-oriented themes. The primary system plays an important role, where the good son or the good husband role is very important. This role then becomes a good employee.

    The stories reflect that the managers are happy with their families and seek the support of the family members in a crisis or seek the family for comfort and peace.

    The stories translated into organization settings reflect upon the dependency of the individual on the superiors for direction, guidance and support to perform in the organization.

2. The stories depict the personal involvement of the individual to achieve success but experience constraints due to the structure and the hierarchy of the organization.

3. Some of the stories reflected that individuals were comfortable working alone. It suggested working in silos and a loner-syndrome. This implies that left alone these managers can perform well. But as a team or collectively, they do not fully converge or work as a team.

4. Most stories have a resolution and an outcome suggesting that this group would tend to bring closure to the tasks on hand.

5. Some of the stories reflect confusion, which indicates that the managers had actually not mapped out their role and especially the expectations of the organization for their performance. The group also needed to understand the boundaries of their role and organization and how far they could make demands on the system.

6. Stories reflected self-absorption and experience of loss.

7. Some stories reflected fast decisions while others got caught with ideal role models and were unable to take initiatives.

8. Individuals needed to gain acceptance and respect from seniors.

9. Very few stories reflected a focus on achievements, accomplishments and successes of the individuals.

10. Work was experienced as a source of stress, which required sustained effort.

Card No. 2 & 6

Middle-Level Managers—2000 onwards

1. Most stories reflected father-son or superior-subordinate themes. The superior has a certain expectation and the subordinate has very different expectations from himself and his own role.

2. Father-son themes also reflect the father in the authority role and the giver of advice, whereas the son is a reluctant recipient who ultimately gives in. Father-son themes also relate to issues of generation gap and coming to terms with understanding and acceptance of each other.

Figure 15: Father-Son Interface

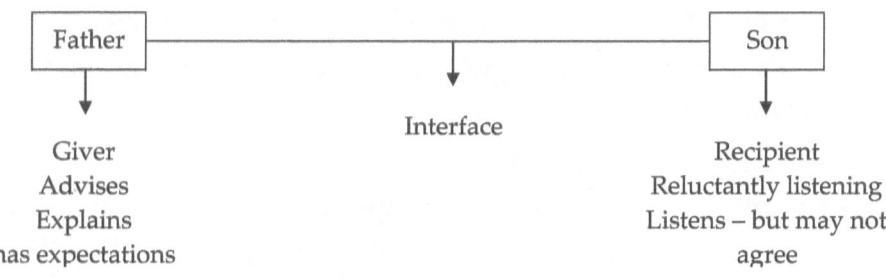

i. The stories reflect the younger person in the passive recipient role.

ii. This means that the subordinates in the organization may find it difficult to take initiatives.

iii. It is the superior who takes decisions, gives direction, and provides advice.

{Adapted from Parikh, I. J/Yadav, V. consultancy (Nov. 2005 – Feb. 2006)}

The above figure shows that there is no interface. Each role is in his bounded space with rigid definitions of one's own and other's roles. As such, there is no movement or resolution of issues.

Card No. 3
Middle-Level Managers—2000 onwards

1. Teamwork is absent. Most of the themes around a situation of the group reflected individuals who are preoccupied, self-absorbed and /or disengaged from the situation and each other.

2. People in groups do not interface across roles or tasks. The individuals seem to be there but not with a purpose or a direction. They interact but do not engage with each other.

3. There were occasional themes of formal discussions. However, overall engagement and involvement were low.

4. Most group themes did not have any resolution and the theme was left with no direction or incomplete agenda.

5. Occasionally, in a group, one individual was engaged with the agenda of focusing on the task. The rest came through as spectators or observers or disconnected.

Essentially, the stories showed that the team works if there is a crisis or when there is a senior person. In the absence of a senior person, the individuals in a group remain self-absorbed, preoccupied and self-centered. A crisis makes individuals alert and they rally around.

Issues Identified by the Middle-Level Managers 2000s

Organizational Issues

1. Managers feel controlled when decisions are delayed or when promotions processes are based on personal likes and dislikes.

2. Seniors often display patronizing attitudes that contribute to feelings of resentment and anxiety in the managers.

3. Managers see themselves as ambitious and hardworking and are looking for growth.

4. Managers are not in charge of their own tasks; they are largely dependent on the seniors.

Managerial Issues

1. Managers have actually not mapped out their role and especially the expectations of the organization for their performance.

2. Managers feel controlled when decisions are delayed or escalations are initiated. They feel they are not valued by their seniors.

3. Managers are not in charge of their own tasks and are largely dependent on their seniors for direction, guidance and support to perform in the organization.

4. Managers are comfortable working in their own space when left alone but as a team or collectively, they do not fully converge or work as a team.

Interface Issues

1. Managers feel anxious and hesitant while interacting with their colleagues, peers and seniors. There is a difficulty in communication among themselves and seniors.

2. Managers are frozen in their space and believe that their seniors' vision is their own vision.

3. Managers feel that they are always instructed and not encouraged to withhold any situation. They are not provided with any direction or guidance.

4. Managers carry unresolved issues and unfulfilled expectations from their seniors.

Table 2: Middle-Level Managers—Differences in decades

1990-1999	2000 Onwards
1. Managers do their jobs with a role and duty-bound focus. They expect the seniors to define their job and roles.	1. Managers see themselves as capable and competent. They take initiatives to define their jobs and roles.
2. Managers carry the baggage of the history of the organization as well as their association with the other role-holders.	2. Managers who have joined as laterals tend to have task-based interfaces. They tend to differentiate between personal and task roles.
3. Managers are mostly involved in routine work and they experience a sense of plateauing.	3. Managers have a logical, rational and functional approach toward their work and keep searching for challenges.
4. The interface space between younger managers and senior managers continues to reflect the social structures of authority and hierarchy.	4. Managers are moving toward professional interface around tasks and performance with their seniors.
5. Peer and collegiate relationships are translated into converging to seniors who become the link across functional relationships.	5. There is a minimum emphasis on teamwork and inter-functional linkages as individuals grapple with working in groups and arriving at task-related decisions.

The above comparison has been drawn between the middle-level managers of the '90s decade and the middle-level managers of the 2000s. The table shows the possible shifts in organizational issues, interface issues and management issues and attitudinal shifts of the middle-level managers.

SYNOPSIS OF CHAPTER 4 - FINDINGS AND CONCLUSIONS FROM THE STORIES: WHAT DO THE STORIES TELL?

C hapter 4 is a continuation of chapter 3. This chapter includes the analysis and interpretation of stories by senior-level managers of the decade of the '90s and senior-level managers belonging to the millennium decade—2000 onwards.

All the stories put together suggested that the universe of managers and the context of the organizations are undergoing immense transformations. This chapter also includes the emerging themes and issues which managers were asked to document as also the issues they were confronting with respect to themselves, their colleagues and the overall organizational structure, etc. These were categorized as managerial, interface and organizational issues. These reflect the location of where the managers experience barriers to cross and the internal inhibitors which do not permit freedom to initiate action or alignment between wished-for and freedom to act or alignment between thoughts, emotions and actions.

Chapter 4 explores what the stories tell and the findings and conclusions drawn from the stories which contribute to managers and the organization being underutilized and confronted to make responses that may not be thought through. Moreover, the rapid changes, when not accompanied by learning and developmental inputs for role change, created stress in the managers as well as the system. With this process, managers and the organization recognized the need to respond to change and to redefine their roles. Chapter 4 highlights the areas of role-taking, the language of the managers, the potentials of the managers which once recognized would contribute to the manager and organization becoming more effective in their job roles, task and performance.

PROFILE OF SENIOR MANAGERS

All managers start from the beginning. They join as young men and women and based on their merit and performance reach higher levels of management. They have a senior management space; they have a position, designation and the responsibility, power and authority which go with the role. Organizations socialize and shape managerial roles in the context, the decade and the era in which the organization is functioning. The role of senior management also causes the characteristics of that era and that decade. The period '60s to '90s had its own coding and caused the special characteristics of the senior managers. Let us present to you the profile of the senior management of those times of the last three decades of the last century.

Senior Managers' Group

Most of the senior managers as a group have been with the organization for a long period. They joined as trainees and over the years have climbed the organization ladder and created a career path for themselves. They are the Tier-I and Senior Managers today. They are home-grown, personally loyal, committed, sincere and conscientious individuals. However, as a group in the context of the organization, they carry a history of relationships with each other which influences their task relationships. In their managerial roles, they retain their functional boundaries, rigid hierarchies and perpetuate the traditional and familial culture of the organization which is anchored in personalized relationships and the history with each other and the organization.

The senior managers are a skilled group and technically competent in their own domain. However, they do not have an organizational perspective. Their silent evaluations and judgments of each other create barriers and inhibitions in functional interfaces. Tensions simmer and occasionally burst into conflicts. Many do not have clarity of the organization's vision. What they largely carry are the targets and numbers. In this, they are hardworking and do produce the numbers. However, the existing interfaces across the senior managers cause delays in decision-making, lack of shared information, poor inter-functional linkages and doing one's own job within the functional space. Openness, an essential criterion rationally accepted and acknowledged as a good working value, however, does not get practiced. The cumulative impact of these is enormous and contributes to immense visible and invisible wastage of time, energy and resources.

In the context of BPR teamwork is an essential process component. In the absence of dialog, negotiation and consultative processes among the group of senior managers, the BPR would not facilitate a dynamic turnaround of the organization. The discussions from the meetings with the managers across levels brought out some significant observations about the senior managers.

1. Senior managers spend a lot of time firefighting, e.g. with the nonavailability of components they have to run around to meet the targets. The quality of components is poor and so there are rejections. In order to meet the targets, there is a lot of follow-up, personal interfaces and running around.

2. Senior managers find it difficult to delegate authority to the subordinates, clearly define managerial responsibility and demand accountability from the subordinates.

3. Senior managers have no time for planning or management as they are bogged down in day-to-day routine operations.

4. Senior managers heading their functions are working as chimneys and silos.

5. Assignments are identified and given but they are not followed up with proper monitoring. There is no track or record of given assignments whether they are completed or thrown by the wayside.

6. Senior managers take on many responsibilities but cannot complete them. They are not held accountable. No demands are made on them.

7. Senior managers carry stress as they are finally accountable.

8. The mindsets of senior managers is changing but at a slow pace.

9. Senior managers work very hard for crisis management. The belief is that things get done or decisions are given only when there is a crisis. So every task and activity is crisis-prone.

10. The senior managers have internalized their earlier bosses to focus on the routine and day-to-day operations and withhold their innovativeness and creativity.

11. Senior managers compete with each other to have access and contact with top management.

12. Senior managers have psychologically not registered the changing scenario of the external environment and its threats, opportunities and challenges.

13. There is a tendency and pre-occupation in the senior managers' group to attribute all sources of the problems to others, outside or to the situation of the union and the workers.

14. Senior managers are a devoted group of people.

15. There are no inter-functional linkages nor effective teamwork.

16. Senior managers preach downwards.

17. Senior managers do not articulate the real issues or hidden agendas in the fear of punishment for what they have said or what they have said being held against them.

18. They carry history, animosity and residual issues around personalized relationships that have built up and accumulated over a long period.

19. There is a lack of trust across various levels of the organization.

20. Generally, senior managers remain in the right and appropriate behavior vis-a-vis the top management.

21. A senior manager who works more gets more work while others get away by doing as little as possible.

22. A senior manager who is positive may not get the rewards while a non-working articulate person may get the reward.

23. Senior managers do not have the courage to take a tough stand with the workers. There is a wish to do so but they fear they may not get support from the system.

24. Each function is a kingdom and each one tries to see what is best for his own kingdom and not the empire.

25. Senior managers do not go to each other's cabin and information is not shared.

26. Senior managers stab each other in the back.

The dynamics of existing maps and definitions of a senior manager's role is that of being a good son and an employee of the management and treating the management as parents. They are dutiful and bring their sincerity to the workplace. However, in today's context, this is not adequate and sufficient for the organization to become dynamic. The senior managers need to be aware of the environmental challenges and opportunities, rise from their slumber and respond to the new environment. The need of the hour is that they rise to the new managerial roles and managerial leadership required at the senior-level. They need to set the example to be effective strategic leaders and role models for others to follow.

The senior managers are quite dissatisfied as they feel they are neither recognized nor valued. They believe they have brought their best to the organization and sacrificed their family lives. However, the people down the line perceive the senior managers to have too much control and believe they are the ones who will empower and delegate others down the line. This creates helplessness, shrinkage of role space and disengagement in others. The senior managers do not seek or listen to ideas from others. Often they do not have answers to questions asked by subordinates and/or directions and guidance for emerging critical problems.

The senior managers are expected to restore and support the discipline.

The senior managers fear change as there will be too many demands on them. The long-term planning role of senior managers has been limited.

As a group, the senior managers have been required to be only performers and doers of the decisions taken at the top. They have played this role effectively and well when they were middle managers as well. The new role demanded of them requires a managerial leadership perspective which will equip them to take up the role of senior managers individually and collectively.

Figure 16: Senior Managers' Task-Role Interface

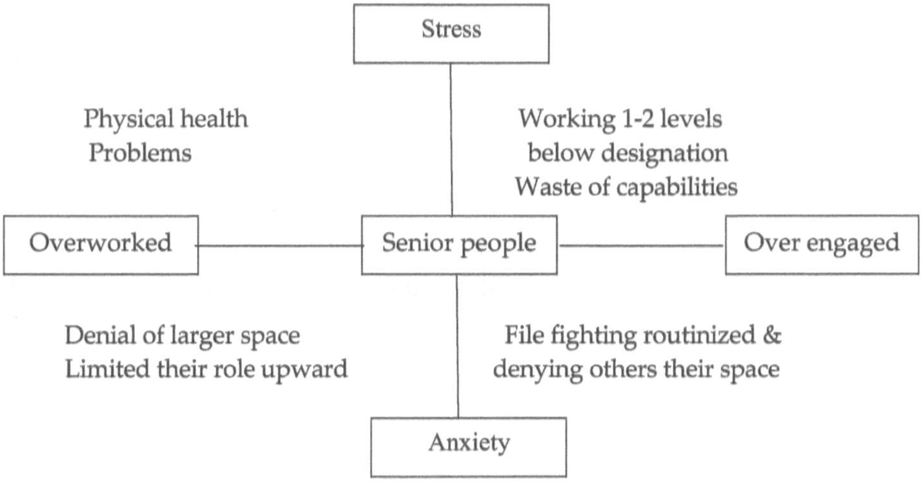

129

i. The senior managers are overworked and experience stress. This manifests in physical health problems

ii. The overengagement with routine jobs makes them work one-to-two levels below their designation.

iii. The senior managers deny larger roles for themselves as they work only with fail-sage practices

iv. Their overengagement is with firefighting of the routinized tasks. This undermines others' role space

{Parikh, Indira .J, Organization Cultural Transformation Process, A Study of Mahindra & Mahindra Tractor Division, Indian Institute of Management (Ahmedabad), (Jan – May 1997)}

The discussions brought out some of the constituents of the senior managers' role required of them.

Senior-Level Managers—1990's

1. There is incongruence between organizational needs and employee-needs as there is confusion with respect to understanding what the managers are seeking. A degree of ambiguity and uncertainty is present with respect to job, roles and performance.

   Even when organizational structure has been redesigned without the relevant learning inputs, managers continue to work with the framework of the earlier organizational structure. Sometimes the managers are not clear as to the total structure and functioning of the organization

2. There is a lack of organizational vision or if there is a vision it is on paper and not shared.

3. The managers view their work as routine, repetitive, mechanical and thus monotonous.

4. Many managers appear confident and seek challenges. They are competent. They also carry concerns of success and fear of failure while taking on these challenges.

5. Managers consider themselves as ambitious, hardworking and focused.

6. There is a need for the communication channels to be strengthened—intra/inter-department communication and coordination are lacking. There is hesitation to directly connect to other roles without the intervention of seniors. Seniors feel offended if the managers directly go and deal with inter-departmental or inter-functional issues.

7. Effective team building needs to evolve. There is a tendency to allocate blame on other roles/functions. There is a lack of collective approach in problem-solving—managers are individualistic. Most of them focus on their role and duty alone and fail to take into account of their peers and subordinates or the total organization.

8. The authority interface creates immense residues. When seniors impose their way of doing things, their subordinates accept it but in silent disagreement with them. The interactions between seniors and their juniors are mainly characterized by emotional barrenness. Managers fear that the differences and communication may lead to conflicts and arguments thereby leading to miscommunication. Weightage is given to authority—there is a general belief that resolutions can emerge from leaders (seniors) only.

9. Group meetings are considered to be ineffective—they are often characterized by chaos and confusion. They lack coherence and directions. Managers believed that inter-functional meetings or any meetings are a waste of time. They go to mark their presence.

10. Managers experience the pulls and pushes from the primary and secondary systems and often are caught between multiple roles and multiple systems.

11. There is a need for an objective form of performance appraisal, which is based on professional competence. Managers feel devalued and demotivated with the present, subjective and arbitrary form of appraisal.

12. Managers feel psychologically saturated and have reached a professional plateau.

Content Analysis from Stories

1. There are expectations of personalized interaction with the subordinates, peers and superiors.

2. Managers very often play the role of a spectator/observer. They wait and watch as to the directions the seniors or the organization is taking.

3. Managers are apprehensive about the future of the organization as well as their career paths.

4. Managers see themselves in a period of transition and often live with a feeling of "What could be done!" and "How it would be done."

5. Senior managers are given a large amount of functional and operational space. However, they prefer to work in the earlier limited spaces of their comfort zones.

6. Informal groups are associated with indulgence and freedom and a lack of responsibility. Some managers are responsible and accountable while others tend to push it upward.

Cards No. 1, 4, 5 & 7
Senior-Level Managers from 1990-1999

1. Most of the stories bring about the managers' experiences of the pulls and pushes from two most significant systems of his belonging, viz. home and work.

2. The source of the energy for action in the manager is anchored in the past events, experiences or dreams.

3. There is a predisposition in the managers to play the role of spectator, observer and as such withhold action.

4. There is expectation of personalized relationships in the organization.

5. The individuals are most comfortable in working on their own, in their own space and wait for direction and guidance. Essentially, there is a gap between potentials and translating the potentials into reality.

6. There is a strong need in the individuals to be in control and in charge of situations. This means that he is left alone to do his own job.

7. Some of the employees do not have the experience of real success though there are many who carry aspirations to grow fast.

8. Some employees experience the job as largely routine including the recurrent emergent problems.

9. There are many who have a need to be recognized and for affirmation. They in turn may not be sensitive to their subordinates or others' need for recognition and affirmation from them. Many seek recognition from the top only. They ignore the recognition they get from subordinates and colleagues.

10. Most people reflect themselves as meticulous workers and prefer to work alone.

11. Individuals found it difficult to manage both differences and similarities with others. They lived in the belief of uniqueness.

12. Being good had many interpretations. Similarly, success had the magical feeling of omnipotence. Individuals lived by "All or none" principle. Either they did everything or waited for instructions and encouragement.

13. The managerial component was actually missing. There was a fair degree of job orientation in one's own space.

14. The organization was perceived with the context of idealism, perfectionism and unarticulated expectations. The assumption was the boss should and needs to understand as he is the one who knows what they expect and aspire and as such, should give without their asking or even stating.

15. There were many stories with no resolutions or outcomes. The stories kind of ended in midsentence or faded away into the nothingness of unstated incomplete aspirations.

16. There were no channels to direct the energy of most individuals to reach the destination of achievements and success. As such, there was a strong need felt for leadership roles and qualities and someone who could inspire and mobilize them.

17. Stories reflected a search for direction from the top and as such movement for themselves. There were high expectations from the leadership role.

18. There were issues around self-esteem, confidence and valuing oneself. When something was offered there were feelings of obligation. When nothing was offered there were feelings of neglect.

19. Many stories reflected the past social baggage of hurt and experiences of emotional and are constantly psychologically unfulfilled from significant people in the social system.

20. The individuals were in search of anchoring in themselves so that they do not feel small or crippled.

Cards No. 2 & 6
Senior-Level Managers – from 1990-1999

1. There exists a hierarchical system. There is a predisposition in the employees to fall back on the concept of ownership as such hierarchy and authority and wait for decisions from the owners or top. The subordinates do not believe in arguments or differences and as such

hold back many differences or their own views or ideas. This is further illustrated in the following figure.

Figure 17

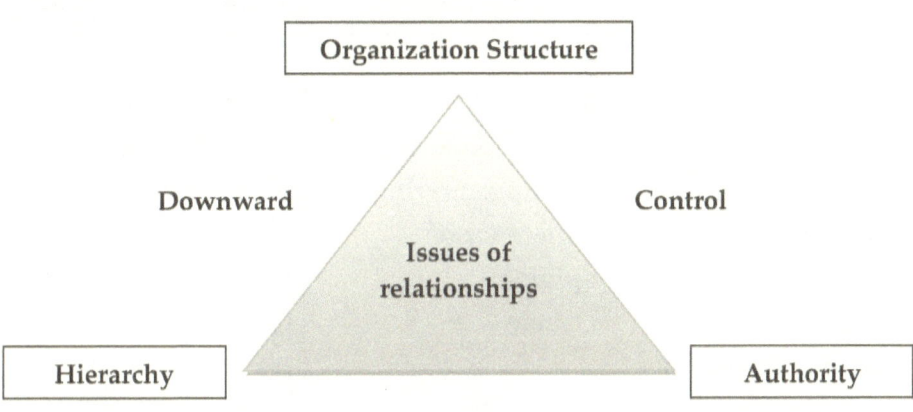

i.   Organizational structure defines the hierarchy and communication downward.

ii. Organizational structure designs the control processes with authority anchored in the owner.

iii. The interplay between hierarchy and authority impacted the social as well as work relationships.

{Adapted from Parikh, I.J, consultancy (Mar. 1999 & Apr. 1999)}

2. Many of the stories have a negative conclusion or resolution in relationships. There is the baggage of regret. The outcome of regret was that it took away all the energy and potentials of individuals. There is either guilt in the self or anger at the other.

3. The stories present the role maps and the nature of the interface between father or the superior as well as the son or the subordinates. The following figure presents the nature of the relationship and the resultant interface.

Table 3 : Interface across Father-Son / Superior-Subordinate

Father Elder Boss	Interface	Son Younger Subordinate
Shouting	Arguing	Dejected
Authoritative	Discussing	Embarrassed
Explaining	Talking on targets	Evaluating the risks
Gives words of	Sets up a meeting	Amazed
wisdom	Difference of	Preoccupied
Advising	opinions	Pensive
Giving guidelines	Debate	Confused
Handing the baton		Listening keenly
Pacifying		May take advice
Asking		worried
Attentive		Sincere, hardworking
Trying to convince		Lack of interest
Suggestions		Frustrated
Full of confidence		Disagree
Full of admiration		Passive
Probing questions		Seeking advice
Understands		Has faith in father
		Avoids confrontation
		Insecure
		Confused about
		career

{Adapted from Parikh, I.J, consultancy (Mar. 1999 & Apr. 1999)}

Most of the words reflect hierarchy, authority, one-way communication and the issues around tasks. The interface is quite predictable which is that each role would stay on his own island. There are no resolutions. The seniors' role in the social system is experienced as largely of controls and a bit of positive relating. However, the interface is neither smooth nor comfortable.

4. When the superior/father is imposing his way of doing things, the subordinate / son accepts it with silent disagreements and doubts. These disagreements are articulated in the form of anger, frustration, and diffidence in some and in the form of sadness in others.

5. There is an expression of sheltering, protecting, nurturing, and caring on the part of superior / father; whereas a feeling of suffocation in terms of less freedom, or no autonomy is expressed by subordinate / son.

6. There are a few stories where the father and the son or the senior and subordinate positively resolve issues by understanding and negotiating whereas in a few stories the outcome is zero or non-successful with no understanding.

7. There is a predisposition in the managers to accept the reality with resentment and carry the baggage of burdened feelings, rather than take an approach of a two-way dialog or communication and sort out issues. The managers have a fear that communication may lead to arguments; therefore nobody takes that risk. The outcome is uncertainty, ambiguity, and finally `marking time', keeping fingers crossed, and waiting for things to change in due course of time. A combination of hope and tolerance is thus reflected.

Card No. 3
Senior-Level Managers – from 1990 - 1999

1. In most stories, the managers hold the view that the concept of a group meeting is a wastage of time. There is an impression of chaos and disagreement associated with meeting in a group. Meetings generally conclude with arguments and no outcome in many stories.

2. Many stories reflect that if superior leads or makes decisions the meetings will conclude on a positive note, indicating weightage given to authority.

3. There are a few stories which perceive group meetings as a ground where sharing of ideas and resolving of problems can be achieved through understanding.

4. When the peer group tries to arrive at a resolution, it ends in chaos and no consensus. The perception is that the resolution has to emerge from a leader who pushes for a solution. The others are then free to critique, disagree or disengage.

5. The individuals in the group stay in their location and make their statements. These statements stand in isolation but there is no relatedness through inter-linkages. No one is responsible for the in-between spaces.

Figures 18 and 19 reflect the dominant group processes in story 3.

Figure 18: Lateral Group Processes

```
          X     X

    X        Group        X

    X        space        X

          X     X
```

{Adapted from Parikh, I.J. consultancy (Sept. 1998)}

Each one is in his space. Each one takes his own stance which is non-negotiable. The discussions do not bring about a review or a change in the perspective. As such, the group space is frozen and there is little or no giving or receiving. Each one is on his island and nothing which is offered can build links, bridges or boats. The group was presented a model to explore and invited to add new dimensions to the group space and group dynamics through taking new initiatives and making relevant and meaningful contributions.

Figure 19: Job, Task, Function and Role Linkages

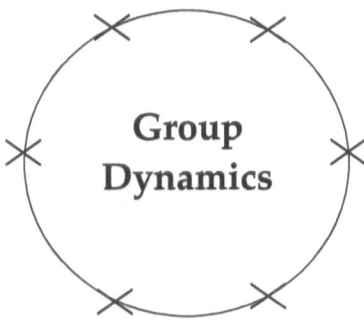

{Adapted from Parikh, I.J. consultancy (Sept. 1998)}

The senior managers' group was invited to identify what processes they could initiate to create a viable and functional group so that decisions by the group for tasks and functions can be made by the group and not evoke a vertical hierarchy. The groups as a senior managers' group have a large amount of operational and functional space where they can take charge and make the decision. In reality, there are a few key decisions related to the overall organization where consultation with top management is essential.

Issues Identified by the Senior-Level Managers—1990S

Organizational Issues

1. Managers worked by the "all or none" principle—either they did everything or waited for guidance and instructions.
2. Managers feel that there is confusion around role-clarity across levels.
3. There is a need to adapt to the changing environment and emerging challenges. Managers were required to manage the shift from traditional managerial roles to professional managerial roles.
4. There is a resistance to change due to cultural crosscurrents within the organization. When there are changes, everything seems to change

Managerial Issues

1. Managers feel the need to have clarity about career planning. Where we are? Where do we wish to be? How should we get there?

2. Managers are resistant to shift from traditional managerial roles to professional managerial roles.

3. Managers feel that communication channels should be strengthened as they are encountering lapses in getting the right information at the right time.

4. Managers feel that the appraisal system is not objective and judgment should be on the basis of professional competence.

Interface Issues

1. Managers have attitudes like "I do better than you" and "Catch me if you can" as there is a lack of trust and confidence across levels.

2. Effective team building has not evolved. There is a tendency to allocate blame on other roles or functions.

3. Delegation of authority and responsibility with accountability is required for managers to take charge.

4. The interface with seniors was a search for clarity as well as directions.

Senior-Level Managers—2000's

1. There is an overengagement with routine affairs and jobs have become monotonous. Managers feel overworked and overengaged and believe that they are not utilizing their potential.

2. There is the absence of teamwork and linkages across roles, departments and functions.

3. Decision-making is centralized. Accountability rests at the top. Senior managers feel overburdened with operational issues and feel they have no time for planning or thinking ahead. They have no time to think and reflect to come up with innovative and creative ways of doing their tasks.

4.   There is a gradual trend toward delegating responsibilities to the subordinates thereby enabling the senior managers to focus on strategic thinking.

5.   Communication is downward and highly authoritative. Subordinates have no space—they are largely in their seniors' space where they play the roles of mere recipients or implementers.

6.   There is no information-sharing down the line.

7.   Interfaces across roles are monitored and controlled by seniors—direct interface across roles does not occur.

8.   The role and style of leadership need to be more open so that senior managers feel they are empowered. There is an urgent need to shift from the autocratic mode of leadership to a more participative and interactive mode.

9.   There is incongruence between the organizational and the employees' vision especially with respect to business, diversification and/or growth.

Content Analysis From Stories

1.   Managers are hardworking, target-oriented and sincere.

2.   Work gets done through relationships—relationships that are personalized or have a long history of association. With roles that are new, it takes a longer time and many follow-ups.

3.   Individuals are preoccupied, self-absorbed and disengaged from the system.

Card No. I, 4, 5 & 7
Senior-Level Managers—2000's

1.   The stories are based on familial themes, which project their dependency on the primary system. This implies that the managers are seeking nurturance in the relationship between the holders of the

system and themselves. In other words, these managers are looking for direction, guidance and support. Once they perceive support or recognition, they perform.

Most of the stories suggest that the managers are still carrying the past residues of the primary system, which they bring to the organization for resolution. They often replay the same situations and enact the same roles.

2. Some of the stories reflect confusion, which indicates that the managers are still anchored and embedded in the traditional role and they are not very sure or clear as to what is their new role. As such, there is confusion around the new role.

3. Some of the stories reflected a loner-syndrome. This implies that left alone, these managers can perform well. But as a team or collectively, they do not fully converge with as a team.

4. Many of the stories reflected a positive focus of working.

5. There are some stories, which are achievement and success-oriented. This gives the individual satisfaction of a job well done.

6. Some stories also reflect hard work. From the stories, these managers come through as target-oriented, sincere and hardworking focused toward success and achievement.

7. Most of the stories suggest that the managers are overengaged and overworked. As a result, they are not utilizing their full potentials.

8. The stories reflect an ongoing work-setting. The work is routine and the individual is a performer and a good employee of the system. However, the outcome in many stories or the result was missing. The stories kind of ended without really ending.

9. Most of the stories depicted a grand vision but the vision was of the manager and not necessarily of the system or the organization.

10. Some of the stories reflect adventure and discovering and experiencing unfamiliar terrains.

11. These managers are ambitious, sincere and hard working. They do have an organizational perspective.

12. Some of the managers are still in search of acceptance.

13. There are many responses, which are the pull of the stimulus rather than managers responding from the self. As such, the managers hold the outside responsible for their actions or non-actions.

14. There is a fear of failure, which inhibits risk-taking or being innovative.

15. Many managers choose to play spectator observer roles.

Card No. 2 & 6
Senior-Level Managers – 2000's

1. The stories are either superior-subordinates or father-son, as such interface issues are hierarchical. The father-son has emotional tonalities whereas the relationship and interface between superior-subordinates are filled with stress and resentment. There are only a few stories reflecting calm and/or positive interfaces between the two role-holders.

2. Most of the stories show that the father is talking and there are no words from the son. The following figures present the nature of the father-son relationship

Figure 20: Role of Father – Son Relationship

i. The dotted line indicates that the father and son are located in their own spaces, which is bounded.
ii. There is a need for communication and interaction to take place.
iii. The interface is not linked.

{Adapted from Parikh, I.J. consultancy (Aug. 2003), consultancy (Aug. 2005), Parikh, I. J/Kollan. B (Aug. 2005)}

Figure 21: Nature of Father-Son Interface

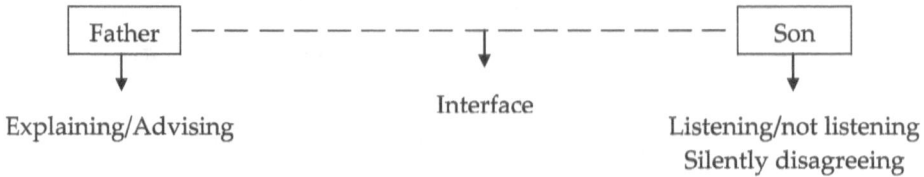

i. During the interface between the father and the son, the role of the father and the role of the son would be different.

ii. The father needs to play the role of an advisor whereas the son would be playing the role of a listener

{Adapted from Parikh, I.J. consultancy (Aug. 2003), consultancy (Aug. 2005), Parikh, I. J/Kollan. B (Aug. 2005), Parikh, I. J/Yadav, V. (Nov. 2005 – Feb. 2006), consultancy (July. 2007)}

3. Most stories are about superior-subordinates relationship. The superior role is emphatic and talking while the subordinate's role was to listen and /or argue.

4. The stories reflect communication downward from the superior to the subordinate but rarely from the subordinate to the superior. The following figure depicts the nature of the interface between the superior and the subordinate

Figure 22: Interface Between Superior and Subordinates

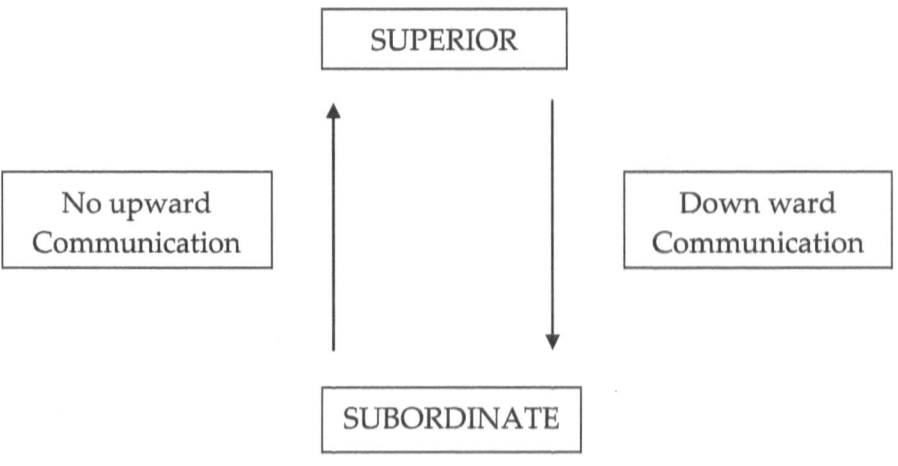

i. In an organization, there is a superior as well as a subordinate.

ii. The nature of the interface of superior with the subordinate would be different.

iii. The superior's communication is always downward whereas the subordinates do not communicate with the superior.

iv. Hence there is no upward communication.

{Adapted from Parikh, I.J. consultancy (Aug. 2003), Parikh, I. J/Kollan. B (Aug. 2005), consultancy (July. 2007)}

5. The stories reflect that the opinion and dreams belong to the father and he is communicating with his son and the son is not able to express his own vision and dreams.

9. Essentially, the father-son or the superior-subordinate stories reflect the baggage of the primary system carried over to the organization.

10. The managerial implications are that the subordinate is a recipient of instructions but does not bring his role to participate. He follows instructions whether he agrees or disagrees. There is no space to dialog or discuss.

11. Most of the stories indicate that the managers show responsibilities and are problem-focused.

12. The subordinates do not carry the mindset of inclusion involvement, participative or being taken into confidence. The reality of the organization may be different but the primary pull is strong. The organization needs to initiate interface processes and persist so that the participation emerges in this group.

13. The superiors are experienced as withholding and not providing any direction or guidance. They instruct what to do but not how to do it.

The interfaces between the father and son and superior and subordinate reflect some characteristic patterns.

The interface between father and son reflects a pattern of defiance, rebellion and a non-negotiable attitude, while the superior-subordinate interface reflects conformity and surrender by the subordinates. However, the stories that both roles of son and subordinates are willing to exile themselves leave the setting and opt out of relationships.

The whole issue around relationship revolves around the legitimacy and illegitimacy of hierarchy and authority exercised by the senior. Although the managers expected guidance and direction they were ambivalent about the authority from the seniors. The belief was that the guidance and direction also took away the manager's autonomy and made him dependent. He merely became a performer. The organizational issue, which the managers explored, was whether the social authority could be exercised in work settings and whether work authority can use emotional power and pressure to make demands on the managers to conform and have personalized expectations. It was difficult for either the father or the son and the superior or the subordinate to explore, discuss, have a dialog to resolve the issues and arrive at a shared understanding.

6. The superior is seen as not listening as well not allowing the subordinates to speak. The communication is largely downward and authoritative. The subordinates do not experience as having their own space. They are largely in the superior's space where they can only be recipients.

7. The stance of the boss is "I know all the answers—both what and how. The subordinates know nothing." As such, achievement and success are inhibited as initiatives are withheld by the subordinates. The accountability is always with the seniors and the subordinates are largely only implementers.

8. Interface across roles are monitored and controlled by the boss. A direct interface for tasks across roles does not occur. Work gets done through relationships, which are personalized or have a long history of associations. Formal functional interfaces focusing on tasks are difficult.

The stories of this card portray the maps, definitions and meanings of groupwork and team spirit. This card like the other two cards reflects the socialization process from the socio-cultural context experienced and internalized by the managers. Similarly, meanings have been given to the culture of the organization around interfaces (Collegial) and inter-linkages across roles, tasks and functions.

Card No. 3
Senior-Level Managers – 2000 onwards

1. Some of the stories reflect that some of the members are friendly and one person in the story is seen as hostile and who is walking out. This indicates that there are linkage and interface issues between the superior and subordinates as in most of the stories it is either a subordinate or colleague who is seen to be walking out.

2. Stories are largely descriptive of the peer group setting. There is very little involvement of the individual to engage with the situation. The group does not commit nor are they taking any stance.

3. The stories describe the geographical layout, the objects and people. The stories suggest a distance and non-engagement with peers and non-involvement in the situation.

4. Most of the stories show that there is a lot of anxiety and stress among the peer group.

5. Each individual in the group is self-absorbed and preoccupied in his own world.

6. The stories reflect that there is no team leader and as such, the managers are immobilized.

Issues Identified by the Senior-Level Managers—2000s

Organizational Issues

1. Managers felt that the organization was initiating too many new activities and priorities. These are then revoked or shifted before their

completion. This results in a sense of confusion with respect to the understanding of the directions and objectives of the organization, subsequently resulting in a waste of time, resources and energy.

2. Many managers are dissatisfied with the high levels of attrition in certain departments. This contributes to stress and recalibration each time.

3. The infrastructure facilities are not available to all the employees in the organization. There are ranks and grades. Some of these are not perks but necessities of worklife.

4. There is a need for aligning with the customer interface. Customers are intelligent and informed. As such the organization needs to address them differently.

Managerial Issues

1. Managers are concerned with the challenges of growth and as such the roles required of them. They expect knowledge inputs for clarity, role inputs for competencies and capabilities and skill inputs for implementations.

2. There is a lot of fear about stating hard facts and reality. The managers who state them are seen as harbingers of bad/negative news. As such, managers share superficial information and do not engage with hardcore difficulty/reality.

3. Managers feel that they are monitored all the time and even misguided by their seniors.

4. There is a need for identifying mentors who will facilitate the managers to navigate the changes which are occurring in the organization.

Interface Issues

1. Interfaces across roles are monitored and controlled by the boss. Direct interfaces for tasks across roles do not occur. Work gets done through relationships, which are personalized or have a long history of associations.

2. Most of the times, the managers do not know the root cause of issues and as a result, they feel that their superiors do not share the information with them

3. The stance of the boss is "I know all the answers – both what and how. The subordinates know nothing." The accountability is always with the seniors and the subordinates are largely only implementers.

4. The superior is seen as not listening as well not allowing the subordinates to speak. The communication is largely downward and authoritative.

Table 4: Senior-level Managers—Differences in decades

1990-1999	2000 Onwards
1. Managers are overfocused on their jobs and lack organizational vision.	1. Managers tend to be goals, objectives and target-driven.
2. Managers feel the need to anchor themselves in their domain roles.	2. Managers have a positive focus on results with a broader understanding of the directions of growth.
3. Managers play the role of a spectator/ observer and there is hesitation to take the initiative to influence upwards in problem-solving	3. Managers are discovering and experimenting with unfamiliar terrains of the complexity of the organization and competitiveness in the market place.
4. Given the changes occurring in both the internal and external environment, managers are hesitant, anxious and apprehensive about the future and their roles in the organization.	4. Managers are grappling with the challenges and expectations with respect to their new role and organizational directions.

1990-1999	2000 Onwards
5. Managers require clarity for their career paths and career planning for their growth.	5. Managers want mentors to identify choices and directions for themselves.

The above comparison has been drawn between the middle-level managers of the 90s-decade and the senior-level managers of the 2000s. The table shows the possible shifts in organizational issues, interface issues and management issues and attitudinal shifts of the senior-level managers.

Findings and Conclusions from the Stories

All the stories put together suggested that:

1. The group is experiencing the stress of taking a bigger role as the expectations and pressures from the top management are increasing.

2. There are gaps in managerial knowledges, attitudes and perspective with the result that the dependency of the subordinate on the superior increases.

3. Most of the interactions are caught between social and work roles. There is a limited clarity regarding the systems, structures and role processes. There are overlaps in their role behavior, which contribute to the confused expectations.

4. These groups of managers have reached a professional plateau and are in search of new meanings. They are reviewing their past roles in the organization and are in search of future direction and redesigned roles.

Figure 23: Managerial Role Space – Potential Interface

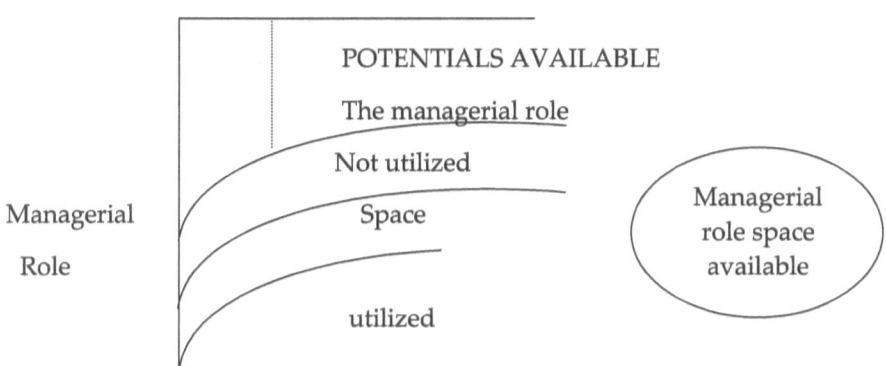

i.	Some managers are capable of anchoring that much only
ii.	Some managers reach there. However, there is a gap in potential achievement and success.
iii.	Managers do not actualize their potentials and talent.
iv.	The role requires initiatives choices, enthusiasm and directions, fast pace growth, ambition and aspirations.

{Adapted from Parikh, I.J. consultancy (Aug. 2003), Parikh, I. J/Kollan. B (Aug. 2005), consultancy (July. 2007)}

5. Essentially the managers tend to underperform and feel inhibited to take limitations and run at a fast pace. Organizationally, the group needs to have a clear-cut picture of the organizational tasks, goals and objectives. Most managers come through as sincere, dedicated individuals putting in hours of work. However, this effort is for routine day-to-day jobs.

Figure 24: Managerial Role Space Interface

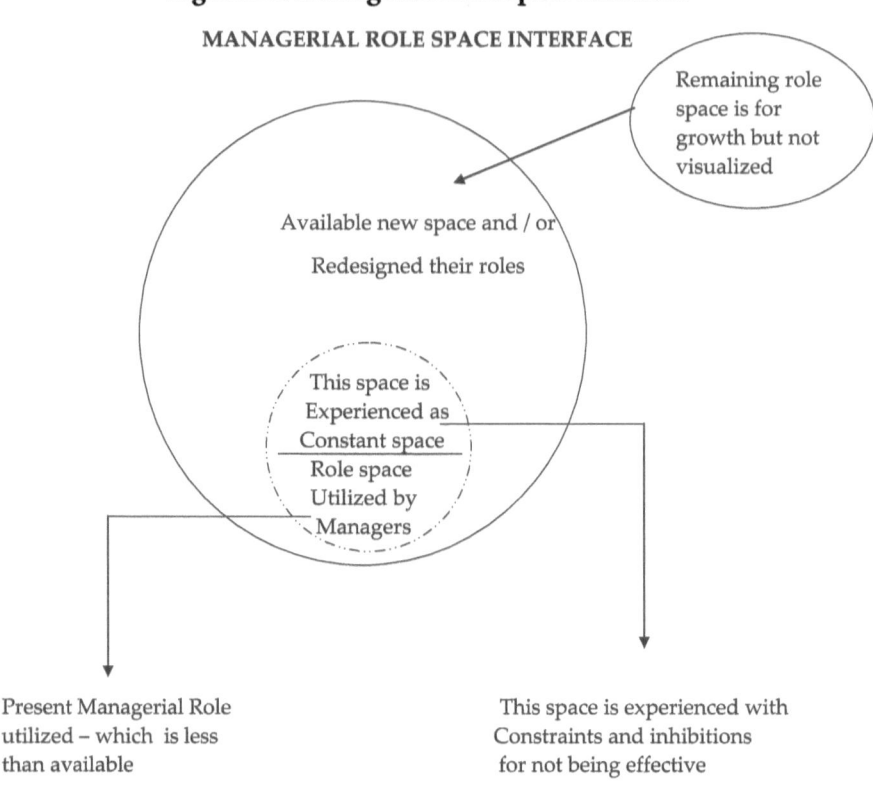

MANAGERIAL ROLE SPACE INTERFACE

Remaining role space is for growth but not visualized

Available new space and / or

Redesigned their roles

This space is Experienced as Constant space Role space Utilized by Managers

Present Managerial Role utilized – which is less than available

This space is experienced with Constraints and inhibitions for not being effective

i.	A manager needs to enlarge the boundary and create a larger role space for himself.
ii.	The group finds it difficult to enlarge the boundaries of the role space.
iii.	Their fear is that if they do it, they will be intruding in someone else's space and territory. And if they do enter someone else's role and functional space, they question on whose terms it shall be.
iv.	Will there be a negotiation or will they have to surrender?

{Adapted from Parikh, I.J. consultancy (Aug. 2005), Parikh, I. J/Kollan. B (Aug. 2005), consultancy (July. 2007)}

6. This dilemma does not release their choice-making process. They wait for being told and do not redefine or redesign their roles. As such, they remain frozen in their stances. The group needs clear-cut directions and a path on which they will walk.

Figure 25: Individual and Collective Energy

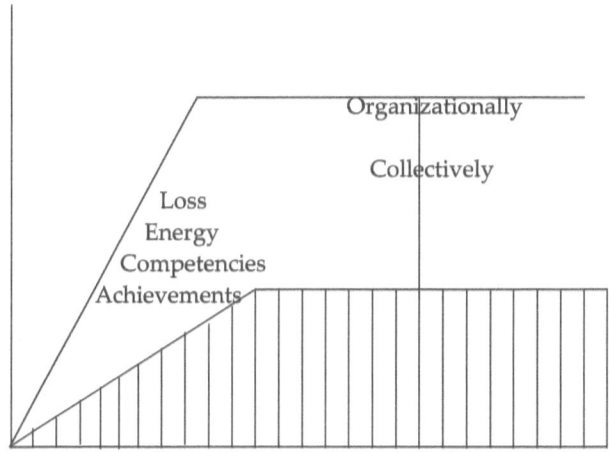

i. Organization experiences loss of energy and it affects the overall achievement individually and collectively.

ii. Collectively managers do not work together.

iii. Managers question their own competencies.

{Adapted from Parikh, I.J. consultancy (Aug. 2003), Parikh, I. J/Kollan. B (Aug. 2005)}

7. Collectively and organizationally so much is at loss. It shows that the group does not work together.

8. The managers are not able to take a position or have an opinion. They are unable to equip themselves to be accountable or motivate people to take initiatives to take responsibility and accountability down the line.

9. As a result, many times the managers find themselves overengaged, overworked and underutilized. They end up doing work one-to-two levels below their designations.

10. Few managers reflect capabilities, competence and foresightedness and come through as goal-oriented. However, they wait for affirmation and recognition from the senior.

11. The interface between the superior and subordinate reflects a lack of initiative and a lack of strategic thinking. There are tight boundaries across each role, which makes it difficult to have a dialog. There are opinions, evaluations and judgments about each other.

12. The group displays a lack of decisions-making and choice-making ability.

13. The interface between the superior and the subordinate does reflect the fact that the superior is not communicating his vision down the line. There is no dialog between the superior and subordinate.

Figure 26: Quality of Superior – Subordinate Interface

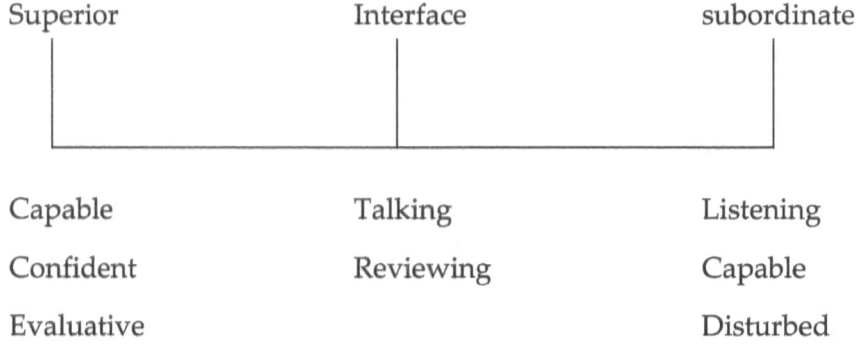

Superior	Interface	subordinate
Capable	Talking	Listening
Confident	Reviewing	Capable
Evaluative		Disturbed

i. These words describe both the father-son and the superior-subordinate interfaces.

ii. Each is a captive in his own space and there is frozenness and inhibition for taking initiatives or reaching out.

iii. Very rarely are the two in a rhythm where one is open and sharing and the other is open and receiving.

{Adapted from Parikh, I.J. consultancy (Aug. 2005), Parikh, I. J/Kollan. B (Aug. 2005), Parikh, I. J/Yadav, V. (Nov. 2005 – Feb. 2006)}

14. The managerial roles taken by the managers have become obsolete in the present context.

15. The managers are caught in managing and balancing the two systems. The thrust for achievements and success at work and assurance of wellbeing and comfort in social systems and roles seem to be difficult.

16. The managers have potentials but the organization or the manager himself has not been able to utilize these potentials.

17. The managers can generate many alternatives but they do not take any firm action. However, the managers need to accept other's expertise as well as constraints to effectively work with each other.

18. The managers do have a purpose but lack the initiatives to implement this purpose.

19. The manager carries the past baggage and residues of relationships while standing at the threshold of the future and waiting for the directions from the seniors.

20. There seems to be an ever-present tension between home and work, which fills the managerial space and roles.

Now let us summarize the dilemmas of the group in the following conceptual frameworks.

Figure 27: Role – System – Interface

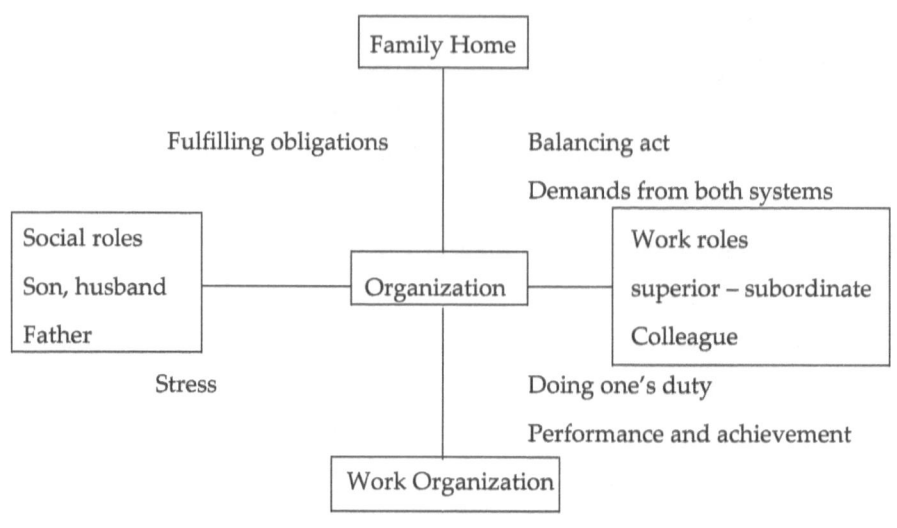

i. Family and home demand social roles from son, husband and father.

ii. The organization demands work roles from superiors, colleagues and subordinates.

iii. Social and work roles mean fulfillment of duty and obligations.

iv. The simultaneous demands from social and work roles demand a balancing act.

v. The managers experience stress and overall pulls and pushes from both systems.

{Adapted from Parikh, I.J., consultancy (Aug. 2003), consultancy (Aug. 2005), Parikh, I. J/Kollan. B (Aug. 2005)}

The investigators explored the sources of the manager's maps and definitions of organization, which they carried and which influenced in their managerial roles. However, the map of the manager's characteristics reflects the new dimensions of role-taking, which is figured out in the following figure.

Figure 28: New Dimensions of Role-Taking

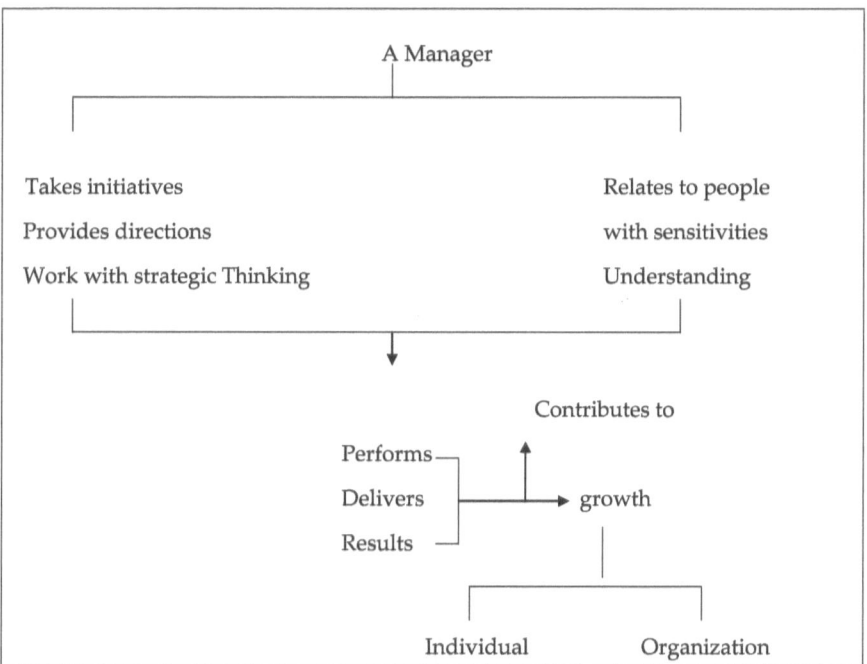

i. With initiative and strategic thinking, a manager can perform to deliver results.

ii. By relating to his team members and providing direction he can motivate them to excel.

iii. A combination of these two factors results in growth for the individual and the organization.

{Adapted from Parikh, I.J. consultancy (Oct. 2004), consultancy (Aug. 2005), Parikh, I. J/Kollan. B (Aug. 2005), Parikh, I. J/Yadav, V. (Nov. 2005 – Feb. 2006)}

Figure 29: Forces Operating on Individuals

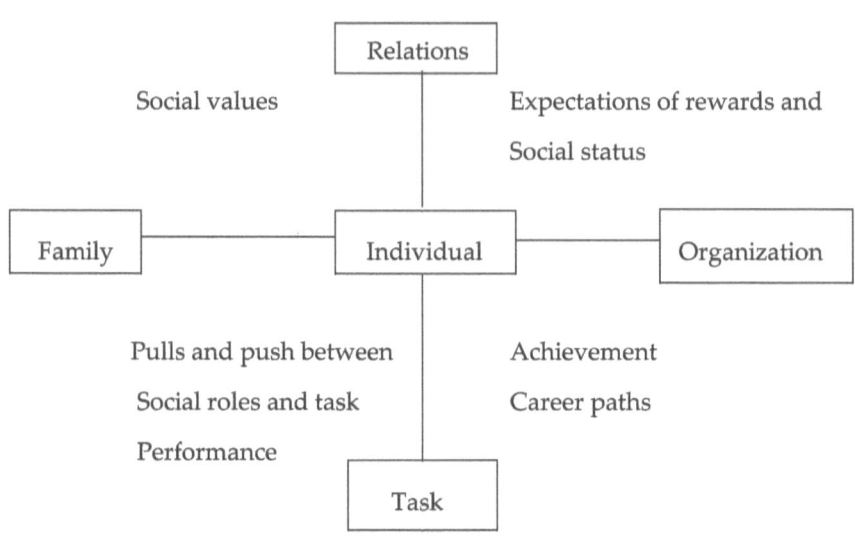

i.   Family fosters social roles.

ii. Social roles and social relations make demands.

iii. The organization has task demands.

iv. Individuals have their own achievements for career paths.

{Adapted from Parikh, I.J. consultancy (Feb. 2002), Parikh, I. J/Kollan. B (Aug. 2005)}

The configuration of primary and secondary systems generates the maps and definitions of people and systems and creates the patterns of interface in the organization.

Each one of us is influenced by the systems we are part of. The family and the relationships influence the individual and subsequently, both the family and the organization do socialization. The individual attempts to balance the two and both the systems make demands on him.

Figure 30: Socialization-Internalization Interface

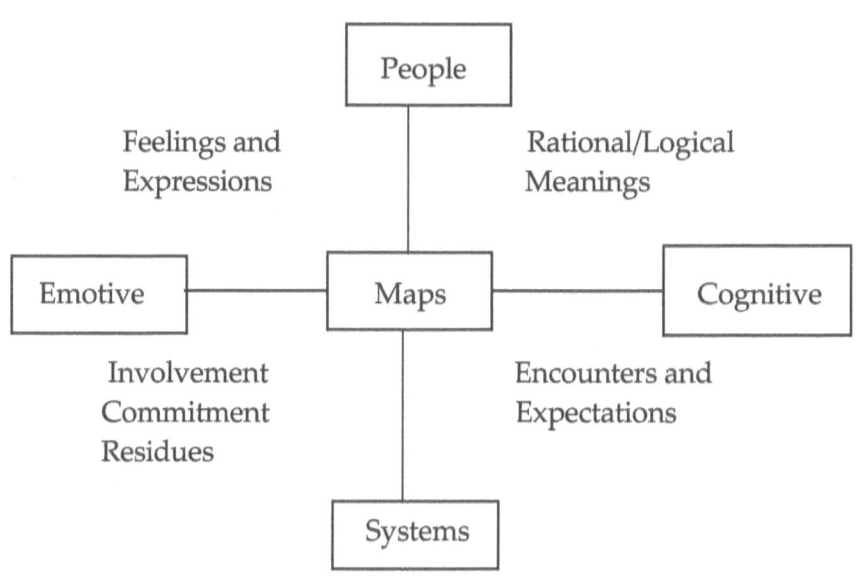

i. Individual experiences people and evolves an emotive component of people.

ii. An individual is part of a system and evolves an emotive component of the system.

iii. Similarly, an individual gives cognitive meaning to his experience of people, and his belonging to the system.

iv. As such, he develops an emotive and cognitive map of people and systems.

{Adapted from Parikh, I.J. consultancy (Feb. 2002), consultancy (Oct. 2004), consultancy (Aug. 2005), Parikh, I. J/Kollan. B (Aug. 2005), Parikh, I. J/Yadav, V. Nov-(Nov. 2005 – Feb. 2006)}

An individual is socialized and the individual internalizes the socialization process, which shapes his role. The socialization process has an experiential component, which consists of an emotive, and a cognitive component. This, in turn, gives birth to emotive and cognitive maps of people and systems.

Figure 31: Emotive and Cognitive Maps

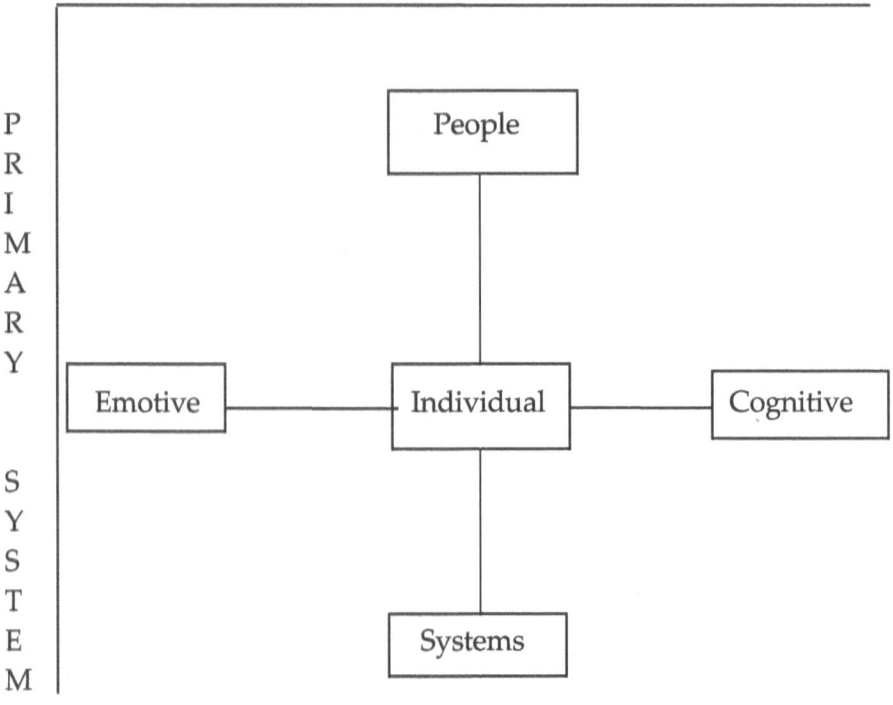

SECONDARY SYSTEM

i. Socialization occurs from the family, which is influenced by society and culture

ii. Socialization occurs from the educational work, and other institutions influenced by the external environment.

iii. An individual internalizes both and develops emotive and cognitive maps of people and systems of both primary and secondary systems.

{Adapted from Parikh, I.J, consultancy (Feb 2002), consultancy (Aug 2005), Parikh, I. J/Kollan. B (Aug. 2005), Parikh, I. J/Yadav, V. (Nov. 2005 – Feb. 2006)}

The family socializes every child into a socially desirable role. The family is influenced by society and culture. All this put together is the primary system of the individual. The individual encounters and experiences the significant people in the primary system and gives meaning to these experiences. The experiences also arouse emotions and feelings. As such, this internalization of experiences gives rise to emotive maps and definitions of people and systems. Similarly, as the child grows, he learns the language and starts giving meaning to the experiences and feelings of the encounters with people and systems. These crystallize into cognitive maps and definitions of people and systems.

As the individual enters the secondary institutions of education, external environment, and work, the secondary institutions also socialize the individuals into desired role behavior for the respective institutions. Thus, the individual acquires an emotive and cognitive map of people and systems of the secondary system.

However, this is not sufficient for the individual. Carrying the emotive and cognitive maps and definitions of people and secondary systems does not permit the individual to respond with his own identity.

The individual translates emotive and cognitive maps and definitions of people and both the primary and secondary systems into emotions and then takes a role vis-a-vis the people and systems. These are the emergent maps and definitions, which include the role and the self of the individual and give shapes to the interfaces in the secondary system viz., the organization. The new configuration of the maps and definition of people and system as crystallized by the identity then determines both the social and work interfaces.

Many of the organizations reflected the processes of transformations occurring in the organization, which put new demands on managerial roles. The managers recognized that both the external and internal environments of the organization are changing at a rapid pace and that the organization is responding to that change. This response also requires that they redefine their roles. For these redefinitions, they need to learn and invest in themselves.

SYNOPSIS OF CHAPTER 5 - ORGANIZATIONAL MATURITY PERSPECTIVE FOR TOMORROW

With the upheaval in the business environment of the organization from the seventies to the nineties, organizations began to go through various stages and phases of growth and transformations. This chapter takes account of those challenges for managers which include aligning the functional tasks, role competencies to manage the dilemmas and pulls and pushes of the primary and secondary systems. The challenges are for leaders which include fostering the growth of the organization to create a global presence. The challenges are for organizations which include shifting from social structures to professionally driven structures. The challenges are for today and tomorrow and what are the lessons learned from them for managers, for leaders and for organizations?

Indian organizations have grown. They have also matured as organizations have moved from social transactions of personal and affinitive relationships to more task-based linkages to perform their roles. The understanding has evolved that tasks are interlinked and so the roles must inter-link whether there is acceptance of each other or not. This has been a major shift in the maps and definitions of roles and organizations as held by managers in the organizations. Similarly, technological innovations and the IT sector created an environment where the young knew more of the functional technology than the seniors. This created a dynamics of upsetting the social equilibrium between the social roles of the older and the younger and the senior and the junior. The third critical dimension which impacted all these transformations was that the elders and the seniors with their age and experience were not the source of information and adverse without the controls and/or injunctions.

All these and many more became the landmarks of transformations and the contours of the landscape of economic, business and work environment. The chapter locates the emerging roles required in the organization which need to respond to the emerging challenges and opportunities in a highly competitive and complex national, regional and global environment.

CHAPTER 5

ORGANIZATIONAL MATURITY PERSPECTIVE FOR TOMORROW

Introduction

Indian organizations are complex systems. They simultaneously carry social as well as work dynamics of relationships. One demands an emotional response while the other demands a logical rational response. Employees bring with them the social maps and definitions as well as work and organizational maps and definitions of roles and relationships. At some point in time, the fine line and the boundary between the social system and work system get diffused. The employees start to bring the social dynamics of emotions in relationships to the work settings causing immense dysfunctional expectations from work and in their interfaces with other roles. Similarly, in the social system, the logicality and rationality of performance and formal interfaces of work organizations are brought to the social relationships creating distress in the social relationships.

These social dynamics brought in the workspaces impacts as to how the employees perceive organizations and other roles-holders across levels of the organizations as well as relate with them at workspaces. Once this boundary is diffused the behavior starts to reflect the roles the employees choose to play. For example, if the employees believe that workspaces are like family and the workplace is their second home, they start to display the behavior of children. So they acquire freedom or sulk, pout, feel hurt by feeling discriminated, deprived, denied and any demands for work-related issues bring out feelings of rejection. They then want to be pacified and helped to reengage with work in a meaningful manner. The concept of family-at-work-spaces is eulogized in the Indian organizations, often leading to confusion in the organization and role-holders as to when to be family and when to be productive, efficient, and effective and a dynamic work organization managing the competitive market place and the complex business environment.

The stories have been one methodology through which we have tried to understand the deeply embedded processes of socialization by both the social system and the work organizations. We have attempted to explore the managerial maps, roles and definitions of work organizations as held by the employees focusing on their concept of work, relationships and interfaces across levels. We have also attempted to explore how the employees perceive and experience issues of their work at their own job, task and performance, issues arising in interfaces and at the level of the organization.

The focus of this exploration has been to discover responses and responsiveness so as to evolve a professional orientation anchored in excellence in the managers. This was also to understand what and why Indian managers in specific and employees in general, knowing fully what is required to perform and how the performance is required, do not often do full justice to work even if they wish to. This understanding would provide answers to identify those processes at the individual, group and organizational level so as to introduce those processes and practices of working in the organizations.

What constitutes the patterns of Indian organizations?

1. Indian organizations have responded to the toughest challenges of the business environment. Indian organizations have always had to compete at the international level with the historically existing multinational organizations that have worked with formal structures of organizations and the freedom to govern

themselves. Indian organizations first dealt with scarcity, then the license raj, then the policy of employment for life, closed economy, open economy and the immense internal diversity and complexity of the country and then the globalization. To respond to this the Indian organizations responded with articulating a vision, learning to formulate both business and people strategy, and designing some of the most relevant and appropriate structures and systems. However, the difficulty is in the implementation process and sustaining the implementation. In the process of implementation, the key role-holders find many constraints and barriers. The pose reflects the administrative barriers, structural and people barriers, and there are many inhibitors and roadblocks. A people society like India there is always social and political forces advocating info out of those who do not follow the policies and guidelines of the system. There are many who will violate the policies and norms and then negotiate for a reduction of the consequences of their action or non-action. The role-holders and the organizations spend hours and hours in this process of negotiation and investigations to let go of the violations of employees. Over time these become precedents and it becomes more and more difficult to enforce the policies which become a solid barrier to introduce change. There is a predisposition for any new initiative to slide back on the old essays of working. Even if the implementation is strengthened, it starts to falter as sustaining the review and monitoring process on accountability becomes difficult. The organizations go through repeated proclamations that the rules and regulations would be followed and strictly adhered to, but very quickly the organizations slide back to the repetition of dysfunctional performances.

2. Indian organizations have grown immensely in the most complex and diverse environment of the country. The formal organization structures and systems borrowed from the west have become

inadequate and insufficient to deal with the internal and external complexity and diversity. The existing organization structures are limited in their scope, inadequate in implementation, and non-responsive to the diversity of employees of the organizations in the recent time plan of their growth but are unable to manage growth in its multiple dimensions. These patterns of coping sap away the vitality and energy of the organizations.

3. The interface between the corporates and the regions, the regions and the units, and the rest with the HR are sometimes caught in a deaf man's dialog. There is mistrust, defiance, passive resistance and feelings of being devalued, undervalued and not being fair and just. These processes freeze the organizations to a pace of growth which is slow and where many employees reach a plateau too soon and too fast as they do not encounter challenges and opportunities. This sometimes contributes to comfort zones and/ or attrition in the organization leading to immense invisible waste of the organization resources. The organizations often become captives of their own practices and then do not know how to find the freedom to take new initiatives.

4. Critical events occur in organizations, some of which are dramatic and some are traumatic. These get etched in the minds of individuals and internalized in the psyche of the organizations generating caution. This contributes to the narrowing of roles and shrinking of spaces to take initiatives by the employees. They get duty and rules bound and give up on their creativity and innovativeness. They take the role of doers and implementers and leave the decisions, choices and initiatives to someone, anyone from the seniors.

5. The history of organizations is held differently by different individuals. Similarly, the history of organizations is held differently by different groups of people. Again, the history of organizations is held differently by the organization's memory

of itself. There are always mixed and multiple interpretations of history as experienced and lived by people especially the employees of organizations, and those with a long history of association. The memories of the experience and their interpretations very often determine the ways of workings and the role performance of the employees. In the threshold of transformation, the very same employees find it very difficult to respond to new initiatives and challenges of the organizations. What they have held as residues of unfair and unjust assessments or inadequate rewards experienced as punishments are all attributed as restraints and constraints of the system.

6. The focus of employees then gets focused on creating boundaries around their role spaces and disowning the space available to them in their role. They withhold their creativity and initiative and wait for the decisions taken by the top. The emphasis on zero-tolerance also takes away any possibility of experimentation and risk-taking ability or to innovate.

7. The organizations have to look outward to respond to the emerging complex scenarios, the competitive market place, the short life span of any products, the need for newer and exciting messages and slogans to entice the market place, and the organization to be in constant flux and change. The focus inwards is important from time to time to pause and reflect on how to mobilize and energize the employees so that they keep pace with the changing scenarios and times.

8. The future of the country and the industry and the organizations is in flux. The trajectory of growth is unknown. As such, the organizations require clarity and choice of new directions they need to create a new path to move to the future, anchoring in the strengths of the organization, mobilization of people's resources and an inspiring leadership to energize the organizations.

9. The leadership, the institution and the governance model need to identify a group of individuals who will focus on the future agenda of the organization, identify the destinations and draw a road map. When there is a group of people visualizing the future and a dialog emerges across the organization, there are chances that new initiatives with innovative and creative approaches will emerge.

Put together, the multiple constituencies of people and the organization simultaneously interact with each other and create an internal organizational dynamics. Each internal subsystem has its own dynamics and this pulls and pushes the organization in many directions. A comprehensive yet distinct and cumulative focus is required across all levels of the organization for the entire organization to experience a coherent direction to which the individual, collective and organization energy gets channelized.

In order to understand the various levels and their roles and as such their working an attempt is made to create specific bounded spaces and roles. This is to understand the clarity and boundaries of each role level. Six levels are categorized[2].

CEO and Corporate Team

i. Institutional and organizational roles where the CEO and corporate team look at the future directions and macro perspectives of the organization.

ii. Managing internal and external business environment of economy, industrial sector and specific or diverse businesses.

iii. Corporate social responsibility and corporate governance anchored in values of the institution and ethics of business transactions

iv. Giving shape to new work culture as transitioning from the existing economy to a global economy

v. Accessibility of CEO and top management to the rest of the organization so that they can hear and see the leaders at the helm.

Top Management Team

i.   Business and people strategies keeping in mind the transforming business environment and the new generation entering the organization.[3]

ii. Arriving at a shared vision and communicating to all the employees of the organization.

iii. Goal and objectives-driven so that there are challenges and opportunities for employees.

iv. Creating landmarks for the organization by the organization's and employees' creativity and innovation.

v.   Enlivening the mission of the organization where the organization and employees are mobilized.

Senior Management Team

i.   Organizational perspective anchored in the excellence of performance.

ii. Resource and talent mobilization for tasks and of employees

iii. Creating mileposts and action initiatives to experience the growth and distance traveled.

iv. Targets and results-focus so that there is the experience of accomplishments and achievements.

v.   Mobilizing human resources through inspiration by leadership.

vi. Deployment of energy to reach new heights through collectivity accepting accountability.

Middle Management Team

I.   Task performance to experience results and satisfaction of a job well done.

---

3   {Parikh, I.J, (1997), Organization Cultural Transformation Process, A study of Mahindra & Mahindra Tractor Division, January – May 1997, Indian Institute of Management, Ahmedabad}

ii. Experience of achievement and success to enhance self-esteem and self-worth

iii. Interdependencies for task, functional and role linkages so that there is a seamless flow of work.

iv. Merit-based appraisals and rewards to experience fair and just systems and transparent systemic processes.

v. Career paths and professional growth so that individuals can benchmark themselves with themselves as well as others.

New Entrants

i. Seek opportunities and challenges for their ambitions, aspirations/achievements.

ii. Strive to reach new destinations with creativity and innovations.

iii. Aspire to take responsibility and accountability.

iv. Are eager to run and carry the flag to the destinations.

v. Enhance their quality of life with the creation of their own family.

Employees, Staff and Workers

i. Improve the quality of life and their children's education.

ii. Sense of belonging so that they can bring their best.

iii. Enhancement of socio-economic status through steady employment.

iv. Celebrations of social festivals through the participation of institutional and organizational events

v. Children's education as a vehicle for future occupation

SUMMARY OF THE BOOK

ll these learning and developmental inputs provide the leadership, the organization, its collectivity and individuals new ways of working. The entire organization responds to the waves of transformation and through collective effort being stability, consistency and rhythm of working. It is in this continuous process as new work culture and work ethos get shaped.

Emerging Work Ethos and Work Culture

Work is an integral part of human existence. Formal work as we know today is a result of industrialization for over two centuries. Formal work organizations are different in different contexts of growth of cultures, societies and nations. When the organizations are founded the nature of organizations reflects a work ethos where employees come from similar contexts and with shared social structures, relationships and belief systems. As the organizations grow in size and number of employees the organization is structured into more formal systems and processes. The relationship and personalized context start to diminish and uniform patterns of behavior and processes begin to emerge and take shapes. This is when the differentiation between emergence of a work ethos and a work culture begins to emerge. The work ethos is different and, the work culture is different. The definitions of work ethos and work culture have been a matter of scholarly debates and writings.

Work Ethos

Ethos is a Greek word meaning "character" that is used to describe the guiding beliefs or ideals that characterize a community, nation, or ideology[3].

"Work Ethos" is a compound expression built on the Greek word "ethos". With the adjective "work" preceding ethos, the expression refers to a person's work ethic. "Work Ethos" is best understood by the more common expression, "work ethics."[4]

Ethics are defined as the conception of what is right and fair conduct or behavior (Carroll, 1991; Freeman & Gilbert, 1988). Ethics can also be equated with the concept of morals—one's ability to choose between right and wrong, good and bad, acceptable and unacceptable (Joyner, B.E; Payne, D; Raiborn, C.A; 2002).[4]

Work Culture

Work culture is a combination of qualities in an organization and its employees that arise from what is generally regarded as appropriate ways to think and act.

The "work culture" of an organization is a product of its history, traditions, values and vision and "a pattern of basic group assumptions that has worked well enough to be considered valid, and therefore, is taught to new members as the correct way to perceive, think and feel."

Desirable work culture includes shared institutional values, priorities, rewards and other practices that foster inclusion, high performance, and commitment, while still allowing diversity in thought and action [Rollins, T & Roberts, D (1998)].

Similarly, leadership roles are different in the ways the leadership plays his role vis-a-vis the directions of the organization and the employees. Managers and employees work and conduct themselves in

---

4   http://en.wikipedia.org/wiki/ethos

    http://wiki.answers.com/Q/Explain_the_term_work_ethos#ixzz20qp02zHQ

ways which are a reflection of their social identity anchored in social structures and systems which shape their primary roles. Each of these interacts with each other and creates a unique configuration of the organization's identity within itself and the organization's image outside in the market place. Organizations are perceived and experienced through their unique identity patterns as well as how the organization governs itself through the value choices it makes for itself in dealing both internally and externally.

In order to understand the ethos of an organization, and the work ethos, contributed by the identity and the role played by the leadership and the employees of the organization as well as the emergence of the organization's identity, the author believed that this was more clearly understood through the projective methodology. For this purpose, TAT was used to focus on the organization as well as the elements contributing to it. Based on the workshop data and the participants' own reflections of how they perceived the managerial interface and the organizational issues, the authors characterized the work ethos and work culture as held and experienced by the managers of the organizations.

The employees of the organization experience the work organization as a social and familial context. Socially the stories and their content reflect this pattern in the junior-level of managers. These individuals are out of educational institutions for not more than 3 to 5 years. They have not internalized the work role fully and their expectations from both the organization and the authority figures are anchored in the social system. They also carry a large burden of the baggage from the family and they have not resolved some of the hierarchy, authority issues of the family. These are expected to be fulfilled by the organization and their seniors. This to a very large extent contributes to the ethos of an organization where the social and emotional expectations are very much anchored in the family and social structures. Individuals struggle hard to be good sons and daughters and tend to sacrifice their personal aspirations in the name of the family and the organization. In that, they play the role of good employees and keep hoping for the affirmation and approvals from their seniors.

As the organization grows in size, products and the number of employees, the organization recruits more and more highly educated professionals who are very much goals, objectives and performance-oriented. Personal relations and relationships are marginalized and the emphasis is on the task linkages and interfaces. The organization then operates in a somewhat fragmented manner. A group of employees continues to foster the known and familiar relationships and get the tasks done, while the other group of professionals struggles to respond to the task requirements and hold in abeyance the relationship and familiarity dimension. In such a context the work ethos of the organization and the work culture of the organization tend to be fragmented.

The workshops for the group of managers and the employees of the organizations identified the need for the future of their organizations and arrive at the quality of work ethos they would like to create and the kind of work culture they would like to give shape to. As each organization comes to that crossroad where they have to make a choice for the directions of growth and take the organization to the next level they can do so without providing the manager the enhanced role-taking skills and attitudes required anchored in a broader perspective of organizational growth. By trial and error, the employees take their roles and perform. However, the performance of both the individual and the organization is at the best part of the whole potentials possible. Some organizations make a choice at such a crossroad to invest in their employees by preparing them for the enhanced and enlarged role which is qualitatively different from the one they have taken before. This choice also shapes the organization's culture as well as contributes to an organization becoming a learning organization. The employees also grow beyond their limited roles and aspire for adding new perspectives to their performance. In such a setting both the employees as well as the organizations continue to renew themselves. The plateau which they arrived at is for a short duration and the movement forward becomes an ongoing process.

This journey of the organization needs to continue to invest in their employees so that there is a constant movement. As the environment changes, businesses change. Leadership trends and new employees keep arriving. Language changes and so do the ways of working like the unending waves hitting the shores. Transformation continues to keep tapping at the door of the organization. The organization needs to be prepared for the waves of transformation to come and deep down remain founded, grounded and stable to withstand and sometimes ride the waves of growth.

Managerial roles in India have yet a long way to go in terms of professional and effective ways to meet the quality, economies of scale to respond to the challenges of the emerging competition. Indian organizations have to learn to dot the 'I's and cross the 'T's as well as have an emphasis on timelines and 100% quality output. For this organizations need to invest in their employees across levels to have coherence and a convergence of efficiency with excellence, punctuality with commitment, competencies with involvement and ownership and openness with initiatives and most important to be assertive for the roles that they are playing.

Emerging Leadership Profile

Challenges for Leaders of Today and Tomorrow

I. Foster growth of the organization to create a global presence.

ii. Align the organization with people to generate and share the wealth.

iii. Take social responsibility and inspire people.

iv. Invite advisors who will share with the organization their research and learning so that the leaders and the organization evolve to create new paths.

v. Be sensitive and aware of cultural, social, familial, relational, emotional and psychological generational, technological and industrial transformations occurring in the country as well as globally and be prepared to be responsive and shaping these transformations.

Emerging Managerial Profile

Challenges for Managers of Today and Tomorrow

i. Foster efficiency and excellence in the organization to have global quality and being proud of making a difference.

ii. Align individual, functional task and role competencies across the organization.

iii. Foster wellbeing of the team and mobilize them to achieve and excel

iv. The role and function to be supportive of interdependencies so that there is an organizational culture of cooperation, collaboration and consensus in the context of transformations.

v. Respond and manage the dilemmas and pulls and pushes of primary and secondary system and help create an equilibrium in their lives and that of their systems of belonging.

Lessons Learned

i. There is a difference in being power centers and position and responsibility centers in the location of the organization.

ii. Organizational growth requires deep roots for the stability and flow of the river for energy. This leads to transformations in the individuals collectively and the organization.

iii. Managers who are sensitive need to inculcate sagacity so as to create a culture of dialog and exploration and understanding of self, others and the system.

iv. Managers need to open their minds to the invisibles and explore so that they become open to multiple perspectives sometimes contradictory perspectives.

REFERENCES

1. Adlakha, V.; Bellur, V.V, The Transfer of Management Know-How: United States Vs. India, Economic Planning, Vol.20, No.2, March/April 1984. P.3-7. 5 pages.

2. Arbose, J, Quality of Working Life in the Third World, International Management, Vol.37, No.10, Oct.1982, P.38-39.

3. Bamel, U.K., Rangnekar, S. & Rastogi, R. (2011). Managerial Effectiveness in Indian Organisations: Reexamining an Instrument in an Indian Context, Research and Practice in Human Resource Management, 19 (1), 69-78

4. Baumgartel, H, Human Factors, Technology Diffusion and National Development, Vol.19, No.3, 1983, P.337-348.

5. Baumgartel, H, Human Factors, Technology Diffusion and National Development, Vol.19, No.3, 1983, P.337-348.

6. Burger, PC.; Doktor.R, Cross-Cultural Analysis of the Structure of Self-Perception Attitudes Among Managers From India, Italy, West Germany and the Netherlands, Management International Review, Vol.16, No.3, 1976, P.71-78.

7. Chatterjee, S.R. & Pearson, C.A.L. (1999), Managerial Work Goals and Organizational Reform: A Survey of Senior Indian Managers, Asia Pacific Journal of Economics and Business, Vol.3 No.1 (June 1999)

8. Chatterjee, S.R & Pearson, C.A.L. (2000), Indian Managers in Transition: Orientations, Work Goals, Values and Ethics, Management International Review; First Quarter 2000; 40, 1; ABI/INFORM Global, pp.81-95

9. Das, G.S.; Singh, P, Managerial Style of Indian Managers-A Profile, ASCI Journal of Management, Vol.7, No.1, Sept.1977, P.1-11.

10. Das T.K. (2001) Training for Changing Managerial Role Behaviour: Experience in a developing country, The Journal of Management Development; 2001; 20, 7/8, ABI/INFORM Global, pg.579

11. Deva, S, Western Conceptualisation of Administrative Development: A critique and an alternative, International Review of Administrative Science, Vol.45, No.1, 1979, P.59-63.

12. Falkenberg, A; Glamheden, H.; Agrawal, N.; Chong, L.-C. (2004), Rediscovering Indian Management

13. Garg, Pulin .K.; Parikh, Indira .J, Managers and Corporate Cultures; the case of Indian Organizations, Management International Review, v26 Fall, 1986 P.50 (17).

14. Garg, Pulin K, and Parikh, Indira J., Crossroads of Culture, Sage Publications, New Delhi, 1995.

15. Garg, Pulin K, and Parikh, Indira J., Profiles in Identity: A Study of Indian Youth at Cross Roads of Culture, Academic Book Center, Ahmedabad, India 1980.

16. Garg, Pulin, K. & Parikh, Indira, J., "Organization Design and Definitions, Indian Society for Individual and Social Development, Vol. 2

17. Hausen, Carol, D., and Kahnweiler, William, M., "Effective Managers: Cultural expectations through stories about work", Journal of Applied Management Studies, 13600796, December 1997, Vol.6., Issues 2.

18. James P. Neelankavil, Mathur. Anil, Zhang Yong (2000), Determinants of Managerial Performance: A Cross-Cultural Comparison of the Perceptions of middle-level Managers in Four Countries, Journal of International Business Studies, Vol. 31, No. 1 (1st Qtr., 2000), pp. 121-140

19. Joyner, Brenda E; Payne, Dinah; Raiborn, Cecily A; (Apr 2002): 113-131, "Building values, business ethics and corporate social responsibility into the developing organization"

20. Parikh, I.J, (1997), Organization Cultural Transformation Process, A study of Mahindra & Mahindra Tractor Division, January – May 1997, Indian Institute of Management, Ahmedabad

21. Parikh, Indira .J, Paradigms of Organizational Leadership, Self Organized Criticality; The Avalanche Effect, Indian Institute of Management, Ahmedabad, W.P.No.98-05-03, May 1998.

22. Parikh, Indira, J., Unpublished consultancy reports, 1980-2006

23. Parikh, Indira. J, Laura Rath, Leadership in Family Owned Organizations, Indian Institute of Management, Ahmedabad, W.P.No.1319, July 1998.

24. Parikh, Indira. J, Organization Development Design and Institution Building. A diagnostic report. An unpublished consultancy, 1995.

25. Parikh, Indira. J, Organizational Development Interventions in Indian Organizations, Indian Institute of Management, Ahmedabad, W.P.No.1320, July 1998.

26. Parikh, Indira.J, A diagnostic study of a family-owned organization. An unpublished research study, 1995.

27. Parikh, Indira.J, A Study on the movement from Entrepreneurship to Industry. An unpublished research study, Indian Institute of Management, Ahmedabad, 1993.

28. Parikh, Indira.J, Structures and Systems: The Issue of Cultural Interface in Indian Organizations, Indian Institute of Management, Ahmedabad, W .P. No.771, November 1988.

29. Parikh, Indira.J, and Farrell, Pauline, Approaches To Women Managers' Training, MDP, COMSEC, London, 1991.

30. Parikh, Indira.J.; and Garg, Pulin. K, "Indian Organizations: Valued Dilemmas in Managerial Roles", In the Management of Organizations for developing countries, R N Kanungo and A M Jeeger (Eds.), Routledge Ltd., London, 1990.

31. Rollins, Thomas. & Roberts Darryl., 1998, Work Culture, Organization Performance and Business Process, http://www.citehr. com/23671-work-culture.html#ixzz20rYtdin6

32. Simonetti, J.L.; Boseman, F.G, The Impact of Market Competition on Organizational Structure and Effectiveness: A Cross-cultural Study, Academy of Management Journal, Vol.18, No.3, Sept.1975, P.631-638.

33. Singh, P.; Das, G, Organizational Culture and its Impact on Commitment to work, ASCI Journal of Management, Vol.6, No.2, March 1977, P.235-239.

34. Sinha, J.B, A Model of Effective Leadership Styles in India, A.N.S. Institute of Social Studies, Patna, India, International Studies Management & Organization, Vol.14, No.2/3, Spring/fall 1984.P.86-98. 13 pages.

35. Small, B.W, How to Transfer Technology, Management Today, Sept.1977, P.191

36. Stahl, D.G, Managerial Effectiveness in Developing Countries, International Review of Administrative Science, Vol.45, No.1, 1979, P.1-5.

37. Tomkins, Silvan. S., The Thematic Apperception Test: The Theory and Technique of Interpretation, Published by Grune and Stratton, Inc., New York, 1947

38. http://en.wikipedia.org/wiki/ethos

39. http://wiki.answers.com/Q/Explain_the_term_work_ethos#ixzz20qp02zHQ

FIGURES ADAPTED FROM

1. Parikh, Indira .J, Inter-Functional Team Building, Group I – Workshop II, Anil Starch Products Ltd, Indian Institute of Management (Ahmedabad), (Apr. 1996)

2. Parikh, Indira .J, Middle Managers Group II, Workshop II, Onida Bombay, Indian Institute of Management (Ahmedabad), (May 1st, 1996)

3. Parikh, Indira .J, Organization Cultural Transformation Process, A Study of Mahindra & Mahindra Tractor Division, Indian Institute of Management (Ahmedabad), (Jan – May 1997)

4. Parikh, Indira .J, Role of Senior Managers & Task Linkages, Cadila Healthcare Limited, SBU – Pharma, KLMDC, Indian Institute of Management (Ahmedabad), Sept. 7th-9th, 1998)

5. Parikh, Indira .J, Workshop for Managerial Effectiveness, Rave Technologies, Indian Institute of Management (Ahmedabad), (Mar. 31st, 1999 & April 3rd, 1999)

6. Parikh, Indira .J, Managerial Role Effectiveness, Module I Workshop, Phase I, Standard Radiators, Indian Institute of Management (Ahmedabad), (Feb. 2002)

7. Parikh, Indira .J, Managerial Role Effectiveness for Senior Managers, Zydus Cadila, Indian Institute of Management (Ahmedabad), (Aug. 23-25, 2003)

8. Parikh, Indira .J, Thematic Appreciation Test for Top Management, Bajaj Tempo Limited, Indian Institute of Management (Ahmedabad), (Oct. 9th- 11th, 2004)

9. Parikh, Indira .J, Managing Growth and Change @ IIM A: Role of Officers, Indian Institute of Management (Ahmedabad), (Aug 4th-6th, 2005)

10. Parikh, Indira .J & Kollan, Bharti, Managerial Role and Interfaces: Some Organizational Issues and Implications through Thematic Apperception Test, Indian Institute of Management (Ahmedabad), (Aug. 2005)

11. Parikh, Indira .J & Yadav, Veena, Change Management Program, Arvind Brands Ltd, Foundation for Liberal & Management Education (FLAME, PUNE), (Nov. 2005 – Feb. 2006)

12. Parikh, Indira .J, General Management Program, T-Systems India Pvt. Ltd, Indian Institute of Management (Ahmedabad), (July 16th-21st, 2007)

TABLES ADAPTED FROM

1. Parikh, I.J, (1997), Organization Cultural Transformation Process, A study of Mahindra & Mahindra Tractor Division, January – May 1997, Indian Institute of Management, Ahmedabad

2. Parikh, Indira .J, Workshop for Managerial Effectiveness, Rave Technologies, Indian Institute of Management (Ahmedabad), (Mar. 31st, 1999 & April 3rd, 1999) (Table no.3)

www.ingramcontent.com/pod-product-compliance
Lightning Source LLC
Chambersburg PA
CBHW021408210526
45463CB00001B/271